GOING HIGHER WITH GOD

INCLUDING

Why God Used Stephen F. Olford
And the
Foreword by Dr. Ted S. Rendall

Dr. E. A. Johnston

DEDICATION

These chapters on the devotional life of the believer are dedicated with deep esteem to my dear friend, the Doctor:

David L. Olford

President, Olford Ministries International, a minister to ministers touching thousands.

Contents

Foreword

As you read this book, be prepared to be counseled, correct-
ed, convicted and challenged concerning your own walk with
God. It is one thing to walk after God (see Deut. 13:4), or to walk
before God (see Gen. 17:1), but think of walking with God!

In these pages E. A. Johnston reminds us that to walk with
God is the believer's privilege to be enjoyed. God not only rec-
onciles us to Himself but invites us to walk with Him in friendship and fellowship.

From Scripture and Christian biography we are shown how
men and women responded to God's invitation and walked
with Him. An unknown poet expressed the truth this way:

> To walk with God, oh, fellowship divine!
> Man's highest state on earth—Lord, be it mine!
> With Thee, may I a close communion hold;
> To Thee, the deep recesses of my heart unfold.[1]

But more than that: throughout Dr. Johnston's study we are
shown that to walk with God must be the believer's passion.
Other voices will tempt us to leave His side, but we must be
resolute in our resolve to walk with Him. You cannot read very
far into this little book without discovering that to walk with
God there is a price to be paid, not in the sense that we can pur-
chase the privilege of walking with the God of heaven and earth
through any merit that we have. The walk with God that is offered to us is available and achievable only through God's grace.

---

1   Al Bryant, <u>Sourcebook of Poetry</u>. (GrandRapids: Zondervan, 1968) p. 315.

But in order to walk with Him we must forfeit other pleasures and pursuits that, while they may be legitimate in themselves, rob us of the time we need to cultivate our intimacy with God.

But to walk with God is not to begin a journey where we toss a coin as to which path we should take. Those who walk with God know there is a path to be pursued, and it is known as the highway of holiness (see Isa. 35:8). God commends Levi in these words: *"The law of truth was in his mouth, and injustice was not found on his lips. He walked with Me in peace and equity."* On Levi's life was stamped one word: Holy! And he walked with God.

In that anguished search after God that is recorded for us in Micah 6:6,7 the seeking soul cries out, *"With what shall I come before the Lord and bow myself before the High God?"* The prophet responds by outlining God's requirements: *"He has shown you, O man, what is good: and what does the Lord require of you but to do justly, to love mercy, and to walk humbly with your God"* (6:8). But it is these very requirements that expose our spiritual and moral bankruptcy, so that we are cast on God for such an inward work of His grace and power that we are able to meet His demands. In other words, we must bow at His feet before we can walk by His side.

Long ago Amos the prophet correctly observed: *"Can two walk together unless they are agreed?"*(Amos 3:3). For the repentant sinner agreement begins at the Cross where *"mercy and truth met together, and where righteousness and peace have kissed"* (Ps. 85:10). Calvary marks the beginning of the wonder of walking with God.

Ted S. Rendall
Minister & Professor in Residence
Olford Ministries Intl., Memphis, TN

Introduction

It is our hope that this little book will encourage and enable you to have a closer walk with God. A pursuit of God has its rewards both here and now on earth and in eternity future. The individuals in history who have impacted the world for God are a "Who's Who" of Christianity, each belong to that special group of believers of whom it can be said: they knew their God. Men like Luther, Knox, Wesley, Whitefield, Finney, and Moody each shared a common denominator: a close personal relationship with Jesus Christ. They were extraordinary men because they had an extraordinary prayer life. Their walk with God was much like Enoch the antediluvian of whom it was said, *"And Enoch walked with God"* (Gen. 5:24).

We can learn some valuable lessons from Enoch of old. We see in his life a character that was well pleasing to God and favored by the Almighty—all because he chose to have a closer walk with Him. We, too, can have untold blessings if we do the same! God is waiting for each of us to draw near to Him so He can draw closer to us: *"Draw nigh to God, and he will draw nigh to you"*(Jas. 4:8).It is a promise based on Scripture and to those who exercise it will enter a new walk in life unlike anything else before! Just think of it--the Creator of the universe will deign to draw close to who ever seeks Him in a closer walk; and those persons will experience an encounter with God that will change their lives forever.There are great lessons we can learn from our antediluvian friend! Enoch walked with God and so can you! Through a new walk with God you can be entering the most exciting time of your entire life! Therefore, let us pay close attention to the lessons which need to be heeded as we learn to walk with God.

PART ONE

ENOCH OUR EXAMPLE

"By faith Enoch was translated that he should not see death; and was not found, because God had translated him: for before his translation he had this testimony, that he pleased God" (Hebrews 11:5).

The seventh in Cain's line was Lamech, a polygamist and murderer; and the seventh in Seth's line was Enoch, of whom it is said that 'he pleased God.'Lamech walked in the way of Cain, but Enoch 'walked with God'. The distinction is clean-cut, and the lines move in opposite directions. Here are the Church and the World, separated from one another by deep moral dissimilarity determined by their respective relation to God. What always matters is not that people live and die, but how they do so; and so the Bible is not a book of annals, but of attitudes.

—W. Graham Scroggie

CHAPTER ONE:

AN EXTRAORDINARY LIFE

One can choose to live a life of mediocrity and just barely pass the grade and get by, or one can choose to live a life that is extraordinary and that surpasses anything ever imagined! We are born into different circumstances and environments; some favorable and beneficial to success in life. Others not so fortunate are born into unfavorable circumstances and detrimental environments in life which hinder one's progress and success. Whichever lot is yours one thing about life is true: you can always rise above your circumstances.

Each of us has a God-given ability to succeed. God never creates failures or mistakes. The choices we make in life often determine our destiny. This is true in the carnal secular world as it is true in the spiritual life of the believer. In the secular world we can just be average or ordinary based on our effort or lack of it or we can be singularly superior to the masses and rise to the top in our chosen profession. It is true some personalities are driven more than others: an A-Type personality is far more likely to succeed in business than a Melancholy personality who can cheer up the room just by leaving it! However, no matter how we are wired in our character traits we can achieve the very best that God has for us but it will take effort on our part. There is a price and cost to anything truly worthwhile in life. Those who have gone on to higher education know full well the cost (financial as well as the sacrifice of time spent in study) of pursuing advanced academic degrees. Those who have succeeded in business know the cost and sacrifice often to family time and personal time because of the demands of that business or career. The point is what counts costs; and what costs counts.

One doesn't get to the top of Mount Everest in an elevator. To succeed in anything takes both talent and hard work!

Pursuing God is no different. We tend to view our relationship with God in a totally different way than we do our secular lives. We mistakenly believe that just because we become born-again believers that we will automatically have a walk with God that just grows and grows each day as long as we live without any effort on our part. In reality a walk with God requires just as much effort, time, cost, and sacrifice as anything else in life! If a believer wants to go deeper with God it will require certain well-defined acts on our part. It is true that once we are saved from the condemnation of our sins we are promised a sanctification process in our spiritual lives. This sanctification process is not automatic, similar to the physical growth of a child into an adult.

No, no, no. There are many "old saints" out there who are just as carnal and unfamiliar with the ways of God as when they first became believers forty years ago! Age in itself does not guarantee a close walk with God. In fact, the older one gets the harder it is to maintain that close walk with God! How does one then have a close walk with God? Let us turn to the Bible record and look at the lives of individuals in Scripture who it can be truly said, "they walked with God." Let us first examine our antediluvian friend Enoch.

Enoch was an interesting individual. We can learn much from the account of his life in the Book of Genesis. Let us turn there now. We can find Enoch's story in chapter five verse eighteen. Enoch's father's name was Jared and he lived for eight hundred more years after Enoch was born! We see this in the following Bible verses: *"And Jared lived a hundred and sixty and two years, and he begat Enoch: And Jared lived after he begat Enoch eight hundred years, and begat sons and daughters: And all the days of Jared were nine hundred sixty and two years: and he died"* (Gen. 5:18-20). It is amazing that Enoch's father lived to be 962 years old! Talk about inheriting good genes!

As we read further in our Bible we learn that Enoch had a son named Methuselah. And it is incredible but true that this son Methuselah lived to be the oldest person in the history of mankind: for the Bible tells us that *"And all the days of Methuselah were nine hundred sixty and nine years: and he died."* (Gen. 5:27). Can you imagine a man living to be 969 years old! If they had social security benefits in those days we would not be surprised to learn that he outlived his monthly checks! There is a bloodline here in Enoch's family tree that is truly amazing and it goes all the way back to Adam in the Garden. In fact, Enoch is in line seventh from Adam! Adam lived to be 930 years old (Gen. 5:5) and we can only imagine what conversations transpired between Adam and Enoch!

What wonderful stories young Enoch used to listen to at the feet of the ancient Adam; stories of the Garden, stories of how Adam walked with God in the cool of the Garden of Eden. Exciting stories which would have made the heart of young Enoch burn within him! Such tales! Tales of gold (Gen. 2:11); tales of a unique tree (Gen. 2:17); tales of the naming of the animal kingdom (Gen. 2:19-20); such stories stirred the mind and heart of young Enoch! These conversations with Adam must have put a taste in young Enoch's heart for God—and a longing to be near to God.

There is an extremely interesting fact in Enoch's life that bears noting. It is found in verses twenty-one and twenty-two of chapter five of the Book of Genesis. They read, *"And Enoch lived sixty and five years, and begat Methuselah: And Enoch walked with God after he begat Methuselah three hundred years, and begat sons and daughters."* In other words, Enoch lived the first sixty five years of his life not walking with God. During those years he lived like the world–the antediluvian world at that time was full of evil. In fact it is said of those days, *"And God saw that the wickedness of man was great in the earth, and that every imagination of the thoughts of his heart was only evil continually"* (Gen. 6:5).

Something happened to Enoch in his sixty-fifth year! Perhaps it was the birth of his son Methuselah. Perhaps as he looked at that baby boy he felt blessed by his Creator. His thoughts began to turn toward God and he remembered all the stories he had heard from old Adam about God and the close relationship they shared before The Fall. A light went on in Enoch's heart and his heart of stone became a heart of flesh and he now desired a closer walk with God.

Enoch changed his ways, changed his pattern of life; he began to pursue God unlike any other man before him and his life was transformed and he eventually was translated! We see this from the following Bible verse, *"And Enoch walked with God: and he was not; for God took him."* (Gen. 5:24). How did this occur? Does this mean Enoch did not taste death like other men? Like Elijah did he get transported to heaven without dying? Yes. But this event did not occur because of a ordinary life lived by Enoch. No. The Bible commentator Matthew Henry said of godly Enoch, "Enoch lived like no other man and therefore died like no other man."

But how did this come about? The answer is found in a preceding Bible verse in Genesis. We read, *"And Enoch walked with God after he begat Methuselah three hundred years..."* Do you get it? For three hundred years Enoch walked with God on a daily basis! That is a long time to build and forge a relationship! How do you get a best friend? By spending time with him. The time that Enoch spent with God each day so thrilled his heart he wanted more and more of God with every new morning! He simply could not wait to get into God's presence. He, like the Psalmist David, could say, *"As the hart panteth after the water brooks, so panteth my soul after Thee, O God"* (Ps. 42:1).

The lesson learned from this passage in Genesis is this: Enoch had to make a decision—and that was to follow God in a desperate way. He sought Him, he found Him, he enjoyed Him. The same can be said of God in this instance. God enjoyed Enoch's company! In fact, God began to so enjoy the company of Enoch and the sweet conversation they shared that one day they were out walking and God may have said to Enoch, "Enoch, we have been walking together now for three hundred years. Let us not break up this fellowship with the setting sun of today. Come along Enoch. Let us continue this conversation for now and all eternity–and He took him and *he was not."* God translated his faithful friend to heaven to be with Him for all eternity!

Does this story stir your own heart? Does it make you, like the hart, thirsty for God? You can have that kind of relationship with God this side of eternity. Do you desire to walk with God?

I thirst, but not as once I did,
The vain delights of earth to share;
Thy wounds, Emmanuel, all forbid
That I should seek my pleasure there.

It was the sight of Thy dear cross
That weaned my heart from earthly things,
And taught me to esteem as dross
The mirth of fools and pomp of kings.

—William Cowper

CHAPTER TWO:
BIBLICAL EXAMPLES TO FOLLOW

Just as we looked at the life of Enoch in the previous chapter, we can examine some other Bible characters and learn from them as well!

When one thinks of a man who encountered God and it changed his life one cannot help but think of Moses. Moses, the mighty statesmen of Egypt; Moses, the favored in Pharaoh's household; Moses, the Prince of Egypt! Moses who relied on self and murdered a man and fled into the wilderness of Midian! Moses who went from the palace of Pharaoh to the wasteland of a desert! A prince who became a shepherd and who spent the next forty years of his life tending dumb, smelly sheep until he too smelled just like them! But Moses had an encounter with God and it changed his life!

One day Moses was out with his sheep and he noticed a spectacular sight–a bush that was glowing hot with fire but it was not consumed! The following passage in Scripture tells us this remarkable story:

"Now Moses kept the flock of Jethro his father in law, the priest of Midian: and he led the flock to the backside of the desert, and came to the mountain of God, even to Horeb. And the angel of the LORD appeared unto him in a flame of fire out of the midst of a bush: and he looked, and, behold, the bush burned with fire, and the bush was not consumed. And Moses said, I will now turn aside, and see this great sight, why the bush is not burnt. And when the LORD saw he turned

aside to see, God called unto him out of the midst of the bush, and said, Moses, Moses. And he said, Here am I. And he said, Draw not nigh hither: put off thy shoes from off thy feet, for the place whereon thou standest is holy ground. Moreover he said, I am the God of thy father, the God of Abraham, the God of Isaac, and the God of Jacob. And Moses hid his face; for he was afraid to look upon God." (Ex. 3:1-6).

What an incredible scene! Notice a startling fact from this story: it was not until Moses turned aside that God spoke to him. Moses had to move off the pathway he was on to approach the burning bush.

We have to do the same. To follow God we cannot remain on the path of self-reliance, the path of the world, the path of our own making. No! We too, like Moses, must turn aside and seek God in a new way.

Notice that after Moses has this encounter with God he becomes a new man. His life is completely transformed! He goes on to lead an entire nation out of bondage and witness God part the Red Sea! He goes on to have daily fellowship with God atop the mountain and receives the Ten Commandments! How God blesses Moses! But it is a progression. God did not hand Moses the Ten Commandments right after the burning bush experience. No, God had to test His servant's faithfulness. And God works the same way with us—He delivers us, He changes our lives, He Sanctifies us. As we call upon Him in prayer and seek Him in daily fellowship we can hear God speak to us as He did to the prophet Jeremiah with this promise: *"Call unto me, and I will answer thee, and show thee great and mighty things, which thou knowest not"* (Jer. 33:3).

What an example we have in Moses! We have another example to study and this is a man who is related to Enoch. In fact, the man is Enoch's great-grandson–Noah. Notice what God said to Noah, *"And God looked upon the earth, and, behold, it was corrupt; for all flesh had corrupted his way upon the earth. And God said unto Noah, The end of all flesh is come before me; for the earth is filled with violence through them; and, behold, I will destroy them with the earth. Make thee an ark of gopher wood..."* (Gen. 6:12-14).

We are all familiar with what happens next! God destroys the earth with a flood except Noah and his family. Why did God choose Noah over other men? He may have looked favorably upon him because he was related to Enoch; He may have looked favorably upon him for the following reason as well found in verse eight, *"But Noah found grace in the eyes of the LORD."*

In addition to all this, Noah may have found favor in God's eyes because Noah was a righteous man just like his great-grandfather Enoch. In fact, it is said of Noah, *"and Noah walked with God"* (Gen. 6:9b). Noah was just like his great-granddaddy—he enjoyed a close walk with God as well. Noah *"walked with God."* How wonderful! And look how God spared him and his family!

There are other Bible characters that we too can learn from who shared an intimate relationship with the Creator: Abraham, Joseph, Daniel, David, and many more! The study of the Word of God is rewarding in itself for by the very reading of it we are changed.

When we study the Bible we turn our face toward God and heaven; when we meditate on the Word of God we see the face of Jesus! And when that occurs we relate to the text in 2 Corinthians which states, *"But we all, with open face beholding as in a glass the glory of the Lord, are changed into the same image from glory to glory, even as by the Spirit of the Lord"* (2 Cor. 3:18).

So we have models in the Bible to follow to show us how to have an effective walk with God. We have examples before us in godly men and women of the past who have lived in the light of eternity! We will look at a few in the next chapter.

For true power in prayer, hold nothing back. Be surrendered to Christ. Go all out for Him. Forsake all to follow the Savior. The type of devotion that crowns Christ Lord of all is the kind that He loves to honor. God seems to place a special value on prayer when it costs us something. Those who rise early in the morning enjoy fellowship with the One who likewise arouse early to receive His instructions for the day from His Father. Likewise, those who are in such deadly earnest that they are willing to pray through the night enjoy a power with God that cannot be denied. Prayer that costs nothing is worth nothing; it is simply a by-product of cheap Christianity.

—William MacDonald

CHAPTER THREE

HISTORICAL EXAMPLES TO FOLLOW

There have been noteworthy persons in history who have lived for God in such a distinguishable way that it separated them from the pack. Because of their special walk with God they did big things for God–or rather because of their close relationship with God—He did big things through them! Like Enoch they shared an intimacy with God like few others! God rewarded Enoch for his walk with Him. The Bible has this to say about Enoch and his rewards: *"By faith Enoch was translated that he should not see death; and was not found, because God had translated him: for before his translation he had this testimony, that he pleased God. But without faith it is impossible to please him: for he that cometh to God must believe that he is, and he is a rewarder of them that diligently seek Him"* (Heb. 11:5, 6).

God is *"a rewarder of them that diligently seek Him."* To prove this to be true let us look at how God blessed and rewarded Enoch:

1. Enoch did not see death—he was translated to heaven.
2. Enoch was blessed with a godly bloodline–Noah was his great-grandson.
3. Enoch was given prophetic visions—God revealed future events to him.

Regarding these prophetic visions given to Enoch by God we have the Biblical record that states, *"And Enoch also, the seventh from Adam, prophesied of these, saying, Behold, the Lord cometh with ten thousands of His saints. To execute judgement upon all, and to convince all that are ungodly among them of all their ungodly deeds which they have ungodly committed, and of all their hard speeches which ungodly sinners have spoken against them"* (Jude 1:14, 15).

God will reward any believer who is committed to a close walk with Him. Proof of this is found in the history of the Church. We will briefly look at some outstanding individuals who "turned the world upside down" for God by their lives–their lives of a close walk with God.

From the Eighteenth century we will look at four men who had a close walk with God:

1) John Wesley

Few men have been used of God like John Wesley. The founder of the Methodist Church shook the Church of England in revival in the mid-eighteenth century.

John Wesley said of his life with God:
"I this day enter on my eighty-fifth year. And what cause have I to praise God, as for a thousand spiritual blessings, so for bodily blessings also! ... to my having constantly, for above sixty years, risen at four in the morning? To my constant preaching at five in the morning, for above fifty years?"[1]

Wesley walked with God at four in the morning for above sixty years! Are we willing to make that kind of sacrifice to walk with God? Few are, few do, few get the blessings that accompany such a sacrificial walk with the Master. Next we will look at Wesley's friend:

2) George Whitefield

Few men have done more for God than George Whitefield who was used greatly during the Great Awakening. George Whitefield rose at four in the morning every day of his life to be with God as a Christian. Let us look at how God used this saintly man.

---

1   The Works of John Wesley, Volumes 5 and 6. (Grand Rapids: Baker Books) p. 40.

We will use a page from his daily journal from 1739 when he was only 24 years old, he wrote:

> "Sunday, May 6. Preached this morning in Moorfields to about twenty thousand people, who were very quiet and attentive, and much affected. Went to public worship morning and evening; and, at six, preached at Kennington. Such a sight I never saw before. I believe there were no less than fifty thousand people, and near fourscore coaches, besides great numbers of horses. There was an awful silence amongst them. God gave me great enlargement of heart. I continued my discourse for an hour and a half, and when I returned home, I was filled with such love, peace, and joy, that I cannot express it."[2]

3) Jonathan Edwards

Under Edwards the Great Awakening began in the town of Northampton in New England during the mid-eighteenth century. Edwards was one of America's most intellectually gifted men and shared a walk with God that few possessed. Of his close relationship with God we read:

> "I walked abroad alone in a solitary place in my father's pasture, for contemplation. And as I was walking there, and looking upon the sky and clouds, there came into my mind so sweet a sense of the glorious majesty and grace of God, as I know not how to express. I seemed to see them both in a sweet conjunction; majesty and meekness joined together. It was a sweet and gentle, and holy majesty; and also a majestic meekness; an awful sweetness; a high, and great, and holy gentleness. After this, my sense of divine things gradually increased...There seemed to be, as it were, a calm, sweet cast, or appearance of divine glory, in almost everything....I spent most of my time in thinking of divine things, year after year; often walking alone in the woods and solitary places for meditation, soliloquy, and prayer, and converse with God."[3]

---

2   George Whitefield, <u>George Whitefield's Journals</u>. (Edinburgh: Banner of Truth Trust, 1998) p. 262.

3   David Brainerd, <u>The Life and Diary of David Brainerd</u>. (Grand Rapids: Baker

The last man of the Eighteenth century we will take notice of is Jonathan Edward's friend:

4) David Brainerd

Brainerd, a missionary to the American Indians, left a diary which has transformed and impacted many a Christian. He was a man of prayer who had a close walk with God and literally spent his short life for Christ—dying at the age of 29 in the home of Jonathan Edwards, in Northampton, Mass. Any page of his diary will reveal how close a walk this dear man had with his Master. We see from the following:

> "In the evening, singing hymns with friends, my soul seemed to melt, and in prayer afterwards enjoyed the exercise of faith and was enabled to be fervent in spirit. Found more of God's presence than I have done at any time in my late wearisome journey. Eternity appeared very near; my nature was very weak and seemed ready to be dissolved, the sun declining, and the shadows of the evening drawing on apace. Oh, I longed to fill up the remaining moments all for God! Though my body was so feeble, and wearied with preaching and much private conversation, yet I wanted to sit up all night to do something for God. To God, the giver of these refreshments, be glory for ever and ever. Amen."[4]

Four men. Four saints. Four who walked with God and through whom God used in mighty ways!

We will now focus our attention on four worthies from the Nineteenth century. (There are dozens of examples but we will choose four representative men.) The first is:

1) D. L. Moody

Moody was a simple man who loved his God and believed that "the world has yet to see what God can do with a man completely sold out for him!" God used Moody in remarkable ways

---

Book House, 2001) pp. 16, 17.
    4   David Brainerd, p. 159.

both in America and Great Britain. Thousands came to know the Lord under his mighty ministry which was all backed by a close walk with God.

Of Moody's close walk with God we will look at his own words:

> "I was crying all the time that God would fill me with His Spirit. Well, one day, in the city of New York—oh, what a day!—I cannot describe it. I seldom refer to it; it is almost too sacred an experience to name. Paul had an experience of which he never spoke for fourteen years. I can only say that God revealed Himself to me, and I had such an experience of His love that I had to ask Him to stay His hand. I went to preaching again. The sermons were not different; I did not present any new truths, and yet hundreds were converted. I would not now be placed back where I was before that blessed experience if you should give me all the world–it would be as the small dust of the balance."[5]

Moody entered a closer walk with God and he shook Great Britain with his preaching! Thousands were converted under his powerful ministry.

Another man that had a close walk with God during this same century was:

2) Charles G. Finney

Finney was used of God in mighty revival–The Second Great Awakening. Finney shut himself up in the woods and did not come out until he met God!

Of this experience we have the following account in his own words describing the scene after he returned to his law office from his day in the woods:

---

5   William R. Moody, <u>The Life of Dwight L. Moody</u>. (Murfreesboro: Sword of the Lord Publishers) p. 149.

> "As I went in and shut the door after me, it seemed
> as if I met the Lord Jesus Christ face to face...I received
> a mighty baptism of the Holy Ghost. Without expect-
> ing it, without ever having the thought in my mind
> that there was any such thing for me, without any rec-
> ollection that I had ever heard the thing mentioned by
> any person in the world, at a moment entirely unex-
> pected by me, the Holy Spirit descended upon me in a
> manner that seemed to go through me, body and soul.
> I could feel the impression, like a wave of electricity,
> going through and through me. Indeed it seemed to
> come in waves and waves of liquid love."[6]

Finney went on to be used of God in mighty revivals that swept across the northeastern part of the United States–all because of his deeper experience with God! His book *Lectures On Revival* is one of the most popular books ever printed on the subject of revival. He drew near to God and God drew near to him!

Our next subject is a man from the same century who became the most popular preacher of his day. His church in London, The Metropolitan Tabernacle, was continually packed with 6,000 people to hear him preach; this man was a man who walked closely with God and his name was:

3) Charles H. Spurgeon

Spurgeon was used of God in thousands of conversions and he literally shook the city of London with his preaching–in fact, he became the most popular Baptist preacher in history! Few had the eloquence or impact of Spurgeon. He sought God in a daily walk which characterized his life of prayer. It is said of Spurgeon:

> "It is understandable why Spurgeon attracted so
> much praise. The sheer mountain of work he pro-
> duced through his London years was phenomenal.
> During the nearly four decades of ministry, he added
> over 14,000 new members to his church. Two thousand
> two hundred and forty-one of Spurgeon's sermons
> were published up to the time of his death in 1892....

---

6   Rosell & Dupuis. <u>The Memoirs of Charles G. Finney</u>. (Academie Books) p. 23.

Many consider Spurgeon one of the ten greatest English authors with an estimate of up to 300 million copies of his sermons and books printed. During his life the whole evangelical world seemed to hang on his words; and he is still constantly republished to this day. He became a household word, and remains so to this moment in many evangelical circles. At any rate, there are more books, at least religious works, in print today by Spurgeon—a century after his death—than any living or dead English writing author."[7]

Few men walked with God like Spurgeon and few had such an impact! Our last man of the Nineteenth century was a Scotsman used in revival and known for his holy life of prayer. This man is none other than:

4) Robert Murray M'Cheyne

M'Cheyne was a man who sought God in a daily walk of holiness.

His memoir has been used of God as much as this saintly man's preaching! He had a heart for God like few men and sought God with a passion—few in Scotland had such a close walk with the Master! His diary has impacted many for the kingdom and in it we see how he pursued his God. He writes:

> "June 28 [1832]. Oh for Brainerd's humility and sin-loathing dispositions!"

> "July 22. Had this evening a more complete understanding of that self-emptying and abasement with which it is necessary to come to Christ,—a denying of self, trampling it under foot,—a recognising of the complete righteousness and justice of God, that could do nothing else with us but condemn us utterly, and thrust us down to lowest hell,—a feeling that, even in hell, we should rejoice in His sovereignty, and say that all was rightly done."

---

7   Lewis Drummond, <u>Spurgeon: Prince of Preachers</u>. (Grand Rapids: Kregel Books, 1992) p. 25.

"Feb. 23, Sabbath.—Rose early to seek God, and found Him whom my soul loveth. Who would not rise early to meet such company?"[8]

There were many in the Twentieth century who shared a close walk with God but we will choose four stand-outs to learn from them, so we too can have a closer walk with God. It was said of Enoch that he had a special testimony before man and before God. It was said of him, *"he had this testimony, that he pleased God"* (Heb. 11:5).

The next individuals, three men and one remarkable woman, show how close a mere human can come to the Almighty! First is a special lady by the name of:

1) Corrie Ten Boom

Corrie was imprisoned during World War Two for hiding Jews in her home in Holland—she spent years of torture and horror in a Nazi concentration camp; but through it all her strong faith in God made her persevere these tragic hardships. She had a walk with God that few ever have—her story is truly remarkable! Her walk with God sustained her during such difficult times as she writes about in her book, *The Hiding Place*.

Despite the cruel conditions of the concentration camp Corrie and her sister Betsie shared the love of God with their fellow female prisoners. We read:

"Side by side, in the sanctuary of God's fleas, Betsie and I ministered the word of God to all in the room. We sat by deathbeds that became doorways of heaven. We watched women who had lost everything grow rich in hope. The knitters of Barracks 28 became the praying heart of the vast diseased body that was Ravensbruck, interceding for all in the camp—guards, under Betsie's prodding, as well as prisoners. We

___

8   Andrew Bonar, <u>Memoir and Remains of Robert Murray M'Cheyne</u>. (Edinburgh, Banner of Truth, 1997) pp. 18-23.

prayed beyond the concrete walls for the healing of Germany, of Europe, of the world..."[9]

Our next example of one who walked with God was a man who lived most of his life in the presence of God. Few men were able to pray like this man, fewer still have had the close walk with God that this man had. This man was:

2) E. M. Bounds

Through the many books on prayer that E. M. Bounds wrote millions have been inspired by his close walk with God. Lawyer, pastor, and prayer warrior, Bounds would pray daily from 4 a.m. to 7 a.m. One catches a glimpse of his heart for God in the following:

> "True prayer must be aflame. Christian life and character need to be all on fire. Lack of spiritual heat creates more infidelity than lack of faith. Not to be consumingly interested about the things of heaven, is not to be interested in them at all. The fiery souls are those who conquer in the day of battle, from whom the kingdom of heaven suffereth violence, and who take it by force. The citadel of God is taken only by those, who storm it in dreadful earnestness, who besiege it, with fiery, unabated zeal. Nothing short of being red hot for God, can keep the glow of heaven in our hearts, these chilly days."[10]

Our next subject was a son of a millionaire who forsook every advantage in life to become a missionary to China and Africa. This man labored among the natives in the jungles of Africa with such a sacrificial life that it can only be explained by his close walk with God. Forsaking family, friends, and his inheritance he gave it all to God. The man is:

---

9   Corrie Ten Boom and John and Elizabeth Sherrill, <u>The Hiding Place.</u> (Grand Rapids: Chosen Books) p. 199.

10   E. M. Bounds, <u>The Complete Works of E. M. Bounds</u>. (Grand Rapids: Baker Books, 2004) pp. 31, 32.

3) C. T. Studd

Studd was a man who walked in the presence of God. His biography has inspired thousands and his life has been a godly example for all to follow. Some of the following quotes say much about the man:

"If Jesus Christ be God and died for me, then no sacrifice can be too great for me to make for Him."

> "Some wish to live within the sound
> Of church or chapel bell,
> I want to run a rescue shop
> Within a yard of hell."[11]

C. T. Studd died in Africa literally sacrificing his life for others. He was truly an Enoch-like man!

Our last subject spent of good portion of his life behind bars for his faith. He was a man who walked with God no matter the consequence. His writings have inspired Christians for decades. His time in prison weakened his body and he lived in terrible physical pain until he died.

4) Watchman Nee

Watchman Nee, the spiritual man, understood the impact of the Holy Spirit in the life of the believer. He knew how to walk in faith trusting the Holy Spirit with all.

He writes wisely on prayer in the following:

> "We should not open our mouths too hastily upon approaching God. On the contrary, we first must ask God to show us what and how to pray before we make our request known to Him. Have we not consumed a great deal of time in the past asking for what we wanted? Why not now ask for what God wants. Not what we want but what He wants. If such be the

---

11   Norman Grubb, C. T. Studd: Cricketer & Pioneer. (Fort Washington: Christian Literature Crusade, 2001) p. 166.

case, then the flesh is provided not footing here. It takes a spiritual man to offer true prayer...So that his prayer may not be fleshly but may be effectual in the spiritual domain, the child of God ought to confess his weakness that he does not know how to pray (Rom. 8:26), and petition the Holy Spirit to teach him."[12]

What wonderful examples we have to follow! The lives of men and women of faith need to be studied on a regular basis for there is much to be learned from them. In our next chapter we will take a walk with God. Enoch still has much to teach us as we proceed!

---

12   Watchman Nee, <u>The Spiritual Man in Three Volumes</u>, Volume 2. (Washington: Christian Fellowship Publishers) p. 53.

I am persuaded that I shall obtain the highest amount of present happiness, I shall do most for God's glory and the good of man, and I shall have my fullest reward in eternity, by maintaining a conscience always washed in Christ's blood, by being filled with the Holy Spirit at all times, and by attaining the most entire likeness to Christ in mind, will, and heart, that is possible for a redeemed sinner to attain to in this world.

—Robert Murray M'Cheyne

CHAPTER FOUR:

WALKING WITH GOD— THE BENEFITS

It is difficult to think of walking with God without being reminded of our antediluvian friend—Enoch. Enoch not only walked with God, he pleased Him! We, too, are pleasing in His sight when we walk with Him, and the good news is this: when we walk with God there are certain benefits we receive. We will list these benefits for they are good to remember and encouraging to our hearts!

Of the several benefits to walking with God the first of these is:
• It Is Easy: Anyone can do it!

Walking in itself is easy, even a toddler can do it! Walking requires no special gift or talent. A monkey can walk. Walking is one of the easiest things a person can do (unless physically handicapped). Walking is easy and walking with God is easy. There is nothing complicated about it. It is not an impossible task but an easy one. Anyone can do it!

The second benefit to walking with God is:
• You Do Not Have To Be A Scholar: There are no special exams to take.

God does not require you to be a scholar to walk with Him. One doesn't need any academic degrees to walk with God. You don't have to have a Ph.D to walk with God. In fact, you can be an ABC and walk with Him! No mental greatness is required or genius of any kind. You do not have to go to Bible College or seminary to walk with Him. There are no special exams to take!

The third benefit to walking with God is:
• You Do Not Have To Be An Athlete: No athletic prowess is necessary.

God does not require you to be an athlete to walk with Him. This is no long distance marathon or 5k race. You can be a child and walk with Him or be an elderly saint and walk with Him. No amount of physical endurance is needed. You can be in a wheelchair and walk with Him! No athletic prowess is necessary!

The fourth benefit to walking with God is:
• You Do Not Have To Be Rich: Money is not required.

To walk with God requires no money. It is free. In fact, all the money in the world cannot buy a walk with God. Even the richest man in the world cannot buy a walk with God. God does not need your money. During his earthly ministry Jesus thought so little of money when He had to pay his taxes (tribute to Caesar) he told Peter to go find a coin in a fish's mouth! God owns all the gold and all the cattle on a thousand hills. Walking with Him is free—money is not required!

The fifth benefit to walking with God is:
• You Do Not Have To Be Important: You don't have to be a somebody to walk with Him.

God does not require us to be an important person to access Him. Some earthly kings will only grant access to them by other important people. You don't have to be a "somebody" to walk with Him. In fact, it is often the "nobodies" in life who walk with Him. Those who have walked closest to God have often been unrecognized by the world! You don't have to be a somebody to walk with Him!

The next benefit to walking with God is:
- It Is Enjoyable: It is a supreme joy to walk with Him!

There are few things more enjoyable in life than to walk and have fellowship with the Creator of the Universe! If it is as true for you as it is for me the most enjoyable and joyful times of life are spent in His company. Isn't that true? When you walk in a close relationship with Him there is nothing quite like it. It reminds me of the old hymn, "In the Garden"

> And He walks with me and He talks with me,
> And He tells me I am His own;
> And the joy we share as we tarry there
> None other has ever known.

Walking with God is fun! It is a supreme joy to walk with Him!

The next benefit to walking with God is:
- It Is Exciting: The Christian life is an adventure.

Walking with God is exciting. When you leave the natural and ordinary for the supernatural and extraordinary, life becomes exciting. There are few things in life as exciting as walking with God on the mountaintop. Those mountaintop experiences are the most exciting times of our lives! When you leave the boat and walk out on the water by faith and begin to live in the supernatural and extraordinary you do not want to go back and get into the boat of the ordinary!

Walking with God is thrilling. In fact, the Christian life is an adventure!

We have seen that there are certain benefits to walking with God that each of us can enjoy. As I have mentioned briefly some benefits to walking with God, I would be remiss if I failed to also mention the conditions to walking with God. Let us turn to the next chapter to see what the conditions are to walking with God.

The back door of the church ought to be opened
once a year and give all who have not lived up to its
rules an opportunity to pass out.

Repentance is quitting your meanness. Repentance
is the first conscious movement of the soul from sin
toward God.

A conversion isn't worth anything unless it's a dou-
ble conversion. A man must be converted from something to something.

The Christian who will do things in New York that
he would not do at home is a very poor Christian.

Don't worry about your money. God bless you,
bud, they'll haul you off in a shroud without a pocket—and if it had a pocket your arm would be too stiff
to get into it.
—Sayings of evangelist Sam Jones

CHAPTER FIVE:
WALKING WITH GOD— THE CONDITIONS

Walking with God is easy, free, enjoyable, and exciting. You do not have to be a scholar, an athlete, a rich man, or an important person to walk with God. But there is a price and it was paid in blood. Jesus Christ gives us access to the Father. He is our mercy-seat, sin-bearer and Redeemer—Jesus paid it all.

Walking with God is not open to any person. It is reserved for born-again believers. As there are certain benefits to walking with God, there are also certain conditions. The first is:

- You Must Be Born Again: There is no walking with Him unless you are born again.

In fact, that is the very first condition to walking with God. We are all sinners by birth, *"For all have sinned and come short of the glory of God"* (Rom. 3:23). Therefore we all stand under the condemnation of God ; it is only those who confess Jesus as Saviour and Lord that stand justified before God and have eternal life.

By exercising repentance toward God and faith in Jesus Christ we are saved from the penalty of our sins. This is the only way to have peace with God. *"Therefore being justified by faith, we have peace with God through our Lord Jesus Christ"* (Rom. 5:1).

To be "born again" means to believe and trust in Jesus Christ. First, we must acknowledge that we are sinners in need of a Saviour. Then we must repent of our sins and turn toward God in confession of them. Then we must place our faith in Jesus Christ to save us from our sins. When we do this God forgives us (justifies us) and gives us eternal life (to enjoy Him forever)! We have the promise of God in Scripture: *"For God so loved the world, that he gave His only begotten Son, that whosoever believeth in Him should not perish, but have everlasting life"* (John 3:16).

So the very first step to walking with God is to become "born again." When we do this we have "sonship" with the Father, *"But as many as received him, to them gave he power to become the sons of God, even to them that believe on His name"* (John 1:12).

The next condition to walking with God is this—to walk with God we must:
  • Follow: To walk with God you have to follow.

You cannot lead the way and expect God to follow you. You cannot make a move in one direction and then expect God to come alongside you and bless it. No, no, no. How many times in my own life have I made a move, or decision, without first consulting Him, and it ended in disaster. We have the following example from Scripture in the life of King David and the ark. King David decided that he should take the Ark of the Covenant to Jerusalem. He ordered his servants to transport the ark, but he made his move without first consulting God on how to move the ark. God was displeased with David and a man died because of this. We see this from the following:

> *"And David arose, and went with all the people that were with him from Baale of Judah, to bring up thence the ark of God, whose name is called by the name of the LORD of hosts that dwelleth between the cherubims. And they set the ark of God upon a new cart...";* *"And when they came to Nachon's threshingfloor, Uzzah put forth his hand to the ark of God, and took hold of it; for the oxen shook it. And the anger of the LORD was kindled against Uzzah; and God smote him there for his error; and there he died by the ark of God"* (2 Sam. 6:2,3,6,7).

King David moved the ark before consulting God's written Word which had in it the proper directions for transporting the ark of God. The proper way to move it was to carry it on poles not place it on "a new cart" as David had done. David sinned against the Lord by this error and God showed His displeasure! How many times in our own lives do we do the same? We make a move without first consulting God. Before we make an important move in our life we should first seek His face in prayer and in His written Word. If we desire to walk with God we must learn to follow.

Jesus, in His earthly ministry, said to His disciples, *"Follow Me, and I will make you fishers of men."* He did not say, "I will follow you." He said, "follow Me." And the road He travels is a narrow one and often a demanding one. So if we wish to have an effective walk with God we must learn to follow.

The next condition to walking with God is to:
• Listen: If we are to walk with God we must learn to listen.

The Bible tells us to *"be still and know I am God"* (Ps. 46:10). When we walk with God we must be good listeners. Have you ever had a friend who, when you get together, does all the talking? And mainly talk about themselves for they are their favorite topic of conversation. My wife has a friend who will ask, "How are you?" and when you answer, "Fine", she replies, "Well, enough talk about you; let's talk about me!" Do you know anyone like that? That kind of friendship is one-sided, isn't it? Now I applied this to my own quiet time with the Lord each day–my devotional time in the morning. I had to ask myself, when I walk with God do I do all the talking? Is my prayer time filled mainly with "Me" or "I"? Is my prayer time with God like this: "Lord, bless me today, help me today, heal me today, I want this Lord, I want that Lord." and so on? Is my relationship with God one-sided? Do I rush into my quiet time with Him and do all the talking or do I linger in the garden with Him and allow Him time to speak to me.

So to walk with God effectively we need to listen to what He has to say to us. How can we get on our hearts what is on His heart if we are poor listeners?

Jesus said over and over again, "He who has ears to hear let him hear." He did not say, "Those who have mouths to talk let them talk." He knows we have no trouble talking. We do have trouble hearing Him. We must learn to listen!

So to walk with God we need to follow, listen and:
• Obey: We must be obedient to Him.

This is the next condition to walking with God: obedience. After we follow Him and after we listen to Him, we must obey what He tells us! If we seek God and He tells us to go to the mission field and we fail to go we have disobeyed Him; if we seek Him and He calls us into the ministry and we fail to go we have disobeyed Him; if we seek Him and He tells us plainly to do something and we fail to do it or give it; we have disobeyed Him. Why should He ever bother to reveal His plans and purposes for us again if we never obey what He is telling us?

There is a parable in the Bible about the bad servant who buries his talent in the ground and is rebuked by his Master–what good is a servant who fails to obey the voice of the Master? Our Bible states, *"To obey is better than sacrifice"* (1 Sam. 15:22).

Evan Roberts of the 1904 Welsh revival wrote a letter to a friend late in life and the last lines at the bottom of the letter were written in his hand, "Obedience, obedience, obedience!" Reflecting back on his life Evan Roberts realized that the most important thing a believer can do is to obey.

If God reveals to us what is on his heart and we fail to obey Him it is sin! We're missing the mark. So to walk with God we must be obedient to Him!

There is another condition to walking with God and if we

fail here we fail everywhere! And that is this: to walk effectively with God we must be:

• Holy: To walk with a Holy God we too must be holy.

God is holy. In fact, the Bible says the following about God, *"Thus saith the high and lofty One that inhabiteth eternity, whose name is Holy; I dwell in the high and holy place…"* (Isa. 57:15). His name is Holy. The Bible also states emphatically, *"Can two walk together, except they be agreed?"* (Amos 3:3). If we are to walk with a holy God, we, too, must be holy. We must pursue holiness. We must ask God to give us the grace to be holy. We must rely upon the Holy Spirit to make us holy. The Apostle Paul states, *"This I say then, Walk in the Spirit, and ye shall not fulfill the lust of the flesh"* (Gal. 5:16).

In fact, we are commanded to be holy. We see this in the following passages: *"Sanctify yourselves therefore, and be ye holy: for I am the LORD your God."* (Lev. 20:7). And in the New Testament, *"According as He hath chosen us in Him before the foundation of the world, that we should be holy and without blame before Him in love"* (Eph. 1:4).

That holy saint of Scotland, Robert Murray M'Cheyne, used to pray, "Lord, make me as holy as a saved sinner can be!" So if we are to walk with God we must be holy!

One of the most wonderful blessings of a walk with God through life is this: the more we walk with Him the more we become like Him! In summary, to walk with God means to:

• Be Born Again
• To Follow Him
• To Listen to Him
• To Obey Him
• To Be Holy Like Him

And when all this comes together our lives will never be the same! In the next chapter we will look at why we should walk with God.

Part Two:

Enoch Our Model

"And Enoch walked with God: and he was not; for God took him" (Genesis 5:24).

The late Handley Moule, Bishop of Durham in the Church of England, was a very godly man. One day as he was walking along Princes Street in Edinburgh he approached a corner where a group of Salvation Army workers were conducting an open air meeting. He paused for a moment to listen and one of the young women of the group spoke to him saying, "Sir, are you saved?"

The venerable Bishop looked at her with a kindly smile and twinkling eyes and asked her, "Do you mean...?" Here he used three Greek words which were utterly incomprehensible to her. She showed her ignorance by her stupefaction, and the Bishop continued in English, "Do you mean 'I have been saved,' 'I am being saved,' or 'I shall be saved'?"

True salvation is in all three of these tenses. In the past, the believer has been saved from the penalty of sin; in the present, he is being saved from the power of sin; and in the future, he will be saved from the very presence of sin. If any one of the three were left out, there would be no reality of salvation.

—Donald Grey Barnhouse

CHAPTER SIX

WHY WE SHOULD WALK WITH GOD

In the previous chapters we saw examples of individuals who have walked with God. We have also looked at the benefits and conditions to walking with God. In this chapter we will study why we should walk with God.

It is easy to fall into a Christianity where activity replaces relationship. Allow me to explain. We, as believers, can be busy in Christian service often to the point of exhaustion without really having a vital, intimate relationship with God. We can know our Bibles through a great deal of study and know deep things about theology through head knowledge and still not know our God.

Religion is not an intellectual exercise–it was never meant to be one. So we must ask ourselves this question: "Why should I walk with God?" For an answer let us look at the following story of Duncan Campbell, the man who was used of God so mightily in the revival on the Isle of Lewis in the Hebrides islands off the coast of Scotland in 1949 to 1952.

It was said of that glorious time that "the entire community was saturated with God." People hungered for the Word of God and lingered around the churches long after the service had ended. We see something of this remarkable event from the following:

> "Within a matter of days the whole neighborhood
> was powerfully awakened to eternal realities. Work
> was largely set aside as people became concerned

about their own salvation, or the salvation of friends and neighbors. In homes, barns and loom-sheds, by the roadside or the peatstack, men could be found calling upon God and soon the fire spread to other villages..."[13]

Here is Duncan Campbell's story:

He was in his study early in the morning preparing a message to preach at an upcoming Keswick Convention. At this time in his life he was a Presbyterian pastor. From up in his study he could hear singing down in the parlor below. It was his sixteen year old daughter's voice and she was happily singing a hymn. He went downstairs to listen to her. As she finished singing he asked her a question. He said, "Lassie, what is there to sing about so early in the morning at six o'clock?" She came over and sat on his lap and exclaimed, "Oh, Daddy! I have just spent an hour with Jesus. Isn't Jesus wonderful, Daddy?"

Duncan Campbell thought about that remark. He had been upstairs in his study working on a sermon on holiness when he had first heard his daughter singing downstairs. He asked himself this question, "Can I truly say this morning that Jesus is wonderful to me right now?" He answered himself, "No. I cannot honestly say that." This broke his heart. Then he went back into his study and forced himself upon the floor to pray. He prayed all morning until he felt he had met God. Then he came to this realization: for the last several years, even though he was a busy pastor, he had been in a dry wilderness desert as far as his relationship to God was. He had been "Campbell of revival" and a busy pastor but he had lost the joy of an intimate daily walk with God.

Around this time another incident occurred in his life. He met an elder of a church in Scotland who had in his possession a hand written letter by Robert Murray M'Cheyne to Andrew

---

13   Andrew Woolsey, <u>Channel of Revival: A Biography of Duncan Campbell</u>. (Edinburgh: Faith Mission, 1982) p. 119.

Bonar. The elder allowed Duncan Campbell to read the letter, his eyes fell on these startling words of Robert Murray M'Cheyne: "Dear Andrew, I seem to know Jesus Christ better than any of my earthly relatives." These words startled Duncan Campbell. Could he say of himself that he knew Jesus like that? The Holy Spirit convicted his heart and showed him how far away he had strayed from God. Then Duncan Campbell made the following remark: "I realized then that no amount of labor in the vineyard will make up for neglect of the King Himself!"[14]

This story of Duncan Campbell should challenge each of us as to why we need to develop a more personal relationship with God. It is too easy to become distracted with work and life and neglect the King!

We must pause here and ask ourselves this question: "Is Jesus wonderful to me today?" Can we honestly say that we have a daily walk with God that is vital, intimate, and wonderful? Is He more real to us today than He was yesterday? Do we even have a time which is set apart for meeting God each day? Does He speak to us? Can you, like Moses, say that you have an encounter with God every day? Or do you have "dry eyes" in your prayer time rather than "wet eyes" from a love relationship.

Is Jesus wonderful to you today? If He is not, do not despair–this is a problem that can be fixed.

In the next chapter we will look at some examples of men of whom it can be said, "They walked with God."

---

14   Tape recording of Duncan Campbell, titled, "Walking With God".

That I may know Him: ah, I long to know not just
a Christ of far-gone years ago, nor even reigning on
a heavenly throne, too high and distant to be really
known: I long to know Him closely: this is how—
Alive, and in this ever-pressing "now"; a living One
within my heart this hour, communicating His all-
conquering power, who now no longer lives from me
apart, but shares His resurrection in my heart.
                              —J. Sidlow Baxter

CHAPTER SEVEN

THEY WALKED WITH GOD

There have been men I have known in my life of whom I can say: "He walked with God." Several come to mind.

The first is J. Sidlow Baxter. Sidlow was first and foremost a man of prayer. He knew that the most powerful weapon in the Hand of God was a praying saint!

J. Sidlow Baxter's wife Isa told me that she could hear him down the hall from his study at six o'clock in the morning every day (when he was in his nineties!) praying out loud to God.

Often he would spend an entire day in prayer. Most of his life he arose at 5 a.m. to meet God. Sid would comment, "Imagine, that the Creator of the Universe deigns to meet with little Sidlow Baxter every day in my study!" Sidlow Baxter knew his God.

Upon interviewing friends of Sidlow Baxter the common comment about him was this, "When you heard him preach you felt he had just stepped out of the presence of Jesus and entered the pulpit."

Another man that comes to mind is Stephen F. Olford. Stephen Olford lived a life of holiness better than most men I have ever known. He had on the wall of his study a framed engraving of the words of Robert Murray M'Cheyne, "Lord, make me as holy as a saved sinner can be!"

Stephen Olford sought a life of holiness and he pursued God. When Stephen Olford preached you felt the Hand of God upon him in holy unction! Listening to Stephen Olford convinced you that this was a man who had a close walk with God.

Another man whom I knew that walked closely with God was Adrian Rogers. When you sat with him in his study and he casually talked to you it was obvious that this man had a deep ongoing relationship with God. In fact, he reminded me of Jesus more than any other man I have known. When you spend time with Jesus you become like Him. And Adrian Rogers had become Christ-like by long hours spent in the Master's presence!

So how does one have a consistent walk with God? This will be the focus of this chapter.

To begin with, one must understand the story of the manna. In the Bible there is a story about how the Israelites were being fed with food from heaven in the wilderness. The passage reads:

> *"And when the dew that lay was gone up, behold, upon the face of the wilderness there lay a small round thing, as small as the hoarfrost on the ground. And when the children of Israel saw it, they said one to another, It is manna: for they wist not what it was. And Moses said unto them, This is the bread which the LORD hath given you to eat. This is the thing which the LORD hath commanded, Gather of it every man according to his eating, an omer for every man, according to the number of your persons; take ye every man for them which are in his tents. And the children of Israel did so, and gathered, some more, some less. And when the did mete it with an omer, he that gathered much had nothing over, and he that gathered little had no lack; they gathered every man according to his eating. And Moses said, Let no man leave of it till the morning. Notwithstanding they hearkened not unto Moses; but some of them left of it until the morning, and it bred worms, and stank: and Moses was wroth with them"* (Ex. 16:14-20).

This little story about the manna can teach us much about God. God does not want our leftovers when it comes to spending time with Him. He does not want us to eat His bread one week and let that get us through the rest of the month. He wants to meet us daily. We each must have our "Manna In The Morning" in regard to the daily Quiet Time. In fact, there is a little booklet that Stephen Olford wrote entitled, *Manna in the Morning*, and it deals with how to have a quiet time with God each day. I highly recommend it!

I will give you a personal experience which speaks volumes to our topic. I was driving home from work one day when God spoke to my heart. I had just spent a very busy week in a conference and was literally on the mountaintop with God each day that week. This particular day was a Thursday and I was up late the night before and therefore slept later in the morning and failed to have a quality time with God early that day. During the day I failed miserably in my Christian walk. I felt so bad about it as I drove home I talked to God and asked Him, "Lord, why did I fail so miserably today? I have been on the mountaintop with you all week but today I fell flat on my face in sin. How did it happen, Lord?"

Then in the quiet, still place in my heart, the place where God speaks so directly, I heard a recognizable Voice that answered my question. "You cannot live today on yesterday's experience of ME! You must come to Me fresh everyday." Tears streamed down my face as I drove down the street. I realized I had tried to live today on yesterday's experience of Him and that meant FAILURE. I learned an important lesson that day on walking with God.

How about you? Are you living today on yesterday's (or last Sunday's sermon by your pastor) experience of God? Are you going to Him fresh every day? Perhaps you don't know how to have a effective daily Quiet Time. In the next chapter we will look at how to have a walk with God.

In the Old Testament that life which is steeped in prayer is often described as a walk with God. Enoch walked in assurance, Abraham in perfectness, Elijah in fidelity, the sons of Levi in peace and equity. Or it is spoken of as a dwelling with God, even as Joshua departed not from the Tabernacle; or as certain craftsmen of the olden time abode with a king for his work...But the most familiar, and perhaps the most impressive, description of prayer in the Old Testament, is found in those numerous passages where the life of intercourse with God is spoken of as a waiting upon him.

A great scholar has given a beautiful definition of waiting on God: 'To wait is not merely to remain impassive. It is to expect–to look for with patience, and also with submission.

—David Macintyre

CHAPTER EIGHT

HOW TO WALK WITH GOD

Walking with God is not a complicated process that requires special study and unique ability. Remember, walking with God is easy. In its most simplistic form: we walk and He talks. Though walking with God is not complex it is however a discipline.

One must develop the habit of walking with God. In other words one must develop a daily devotional time.

When we study the life of Christ we must remind ourselves that He is our example. Jesus believed in prayer with the Father, Jesus depended on prayer with the Father, and Jesus exercised prayer with the Father on a daily basis. Before Jesus chose His twelve disciples He spent the night in prayer. We find Jesus seeking his Father early in the morning, *"And in the morning, rising up a great while before day, He went out, and departed into a solitary place, and there prayed"* (Mark 1:35).

If Jesus needed to spend time with the Father each day, how can we be so neglectful? Notice that Jesus sought God "early in the morning," and that He *"departed into a solitary place"* to pray. What time of day should you have your walk with God? The best time is before dawn. At this time there are no distractions, no phones, and other family members are still sleeping. Where do you have your quiet time with God? Usually a place in your home that is quiet, well lit, and where you can read, pray, and write. Let's break these down:

1) Reading

First and foremost, you need a Bible; you can add to this a hymn book; or a Bible commentary or a favorite devotional book. Most of the time spent reading should be in the Bible. I find that the Book of Psalms is a good place to begin—this way our focus is on the majesty of God and worship. We must learn how to meditate upon the Word of God. We should be able to say with the Psalmist, *"I rejoice at Thy word, as one that findeth great spoil"* (Ps. 119:162).

2) Prayer

This is the "Walk with God." But remember, this time is not just a time for you to go over an index card of prayer requests (this can certainly be part of your prayer time but not the main focus). Our main focus during this time is God. We are here to meet Him. If we fail to meet Him we have failed in our prayer time. This is a time where we confess our sins and seek His face with repentance and a contrite heart. We are looking for an "encounter" with the Holy One. When we experience the manifest presence of God in our prayer time there is nothing greater than that experience. For God to dwell with us we must see what His requirements are:

How does one ascend His holy hill? *"Who shall ascend into the hill of the LORD? or who shall stand in His holy place? He that hath clean hands, and a pure heart; who hath not lifted up his soul unto vanity, nor sworn deceitfully. He shall receive the blessing from the LORD, and righteousness from the God of his salvation"* (Ps. 24:3-5).

So if we are to walk with God we must have "clean hands, and a pure heart." We must not have unconfessed sin in our lives. Our sin separates us from God. We must stand on the promise of God that, *"If we confess our sins, He is faithful and just to forgive us our sins, and to cleanse us from all unrighteousness"* (1 Jn. 1:9).

Also, we must be aware of how God reveals who He will dwell with. We find the answer in His written Word: *"Thus saith the high and lofty One that inhabiteth eternity, whose name is Holy; I dwell in the high and holy place, with him also that is of a contrite and humble spirit, to revive the spirit of the humble, and to revive the heart of the contrite ones"* (Isa. 57:15).

What God is saying to us is that He will dwell, walk with us, if our hearts are right and in accord with Him. Therefore, we must guard against pride and self-reliance.

To walk with a Holy God we must be broken and humble. We cannot approach Him with unconfessed sin or a prideful heart. How many prayers rise no further than the ceiling because of this lack of understanding of the nature of God! Our walk with God will be hindered as well if we fail to forgive others who have wronged us. We cannot have an unforgiving heart and expect to Walk with a God who has forgiven us.

So this time of prayer is a time where we are focusing our attention upon God; aligning our hearts with God; and entering the very Presence of God. This should be a time of confessing, seeking, meeting, and rejoicing!

If your prayer time is one where you have "dry eyes" then your prayer time is dry. If your prayer time is one where you have "wet eyes" then your prayer time is alive. One of the most amazing things in life is this knowledge: the Creator of the Universe longs to have our company. He wants us; He wants all of who we are and hope to be. When we fail to have our daily quiet time, our daily encounter with Him, we fail Him. He is disappointed. And we have missed a blessing.

This first part of our day should be the most important part of our day! How can we live our day for the Captain of our soul if we have not received our marching orders from Him? Much of the defeat we suffer spiritually throughout the day could have been avoided if we had spent time alone with Him before our day began! If Jesus had to spend time with the Father each day—and He was divine—how much more important is it for us!

The life of victory over the flesh, the world, and the Devil all begins here in the quiet time as we meet and spend time with God. Walking with Him, listening to Him, enjoying Him! But we must make this a habit, a set routine each day. We must desire His company. And during this time we must not fail to worship Him and thank Him for all He has done in our lives.

A. W. Tozer used to lie on the floor of his study four hours a day just worshiping God. If you have a weak prayer life than you have a weak walk. If you have no sense of God's presence in your life you have a very mediocre life. If God's Sprit does not bear witness with your spirit you may not even be saved! *"For as may as are led by the Spirit of God, they are the sons of God"* (Rom. 8:14).

Walking with God is confessing, seeking, finding, communicating, enjoying, rejoicing. It is a special time between just you and the One who made you and saved you.

3) Writing

You may find that when God speaks to you He has something significant to say! You may not wish to forget it. Having a journal or notepad handy will help you jot down your thoughts and how God spoke to you through prayer, His Written Word, and His Holy Spirit. Writing down what God has spoken to you is a way to keep a record of your walk with Him and a way to go back at a later date and reflect upon how He spoke to you that day.

Once you begin a consistent walk with God you will never want to miss it! What breaks this glorious fellowship is sin. Therefore in the next chapter we will focus our attention on the areas in the believer's life that can cause separation between him and his God. But remember this, once you are a son you stay a son (or daughter). The prodigal son left the home of his father but he never left the heart of his father. He was still a son—though living in sin. When we sin we break fellowship with God but not Sonship. God is waiting expectantly for our return—our confession of those sins. He wants to offer us His forgiveness so we can have that fellowship restored once again. He is a longsuffering, merciful God! His grace is truly amazing! We will also focus on areas where one can go deeper with God.

All sin is against God's sovereignty; all sin is against
  God's nature;
All sin is against God's Name; all sin is against
  God's Word:
All sin is against His Person; all sin is against His
  creation;
All sin is against God's love; all sin is against the
  body and blood of Christ;
 All sin is against God's aspirations for you; but
  most of all—all sin robs God of glory.
                          —Richard Owen Roberts

CHAPTER NINE:

WALKING WITH GOD IN LIGHT AND POWER

Sin breaks our walk with God. Any sin. The size does not matter. It can be a thought, a word, or an action. Allow me to illustrate how our walk with God is clouded over by sin with the following explanation by my late mentor, Dr. Stephen F. Olford. The following is from a letter he sent me explaining this area of sin and how it breaks our fellowship with God. Here now are his words on this very important matter:

> "June 29, 2001.
>
> "Greetings in the precious name of the Lord Jesus...The Discipline of God (Hebrews 12:3-11)-- I believe this passage together with other Scriptures show quite clearly that discipline has to do with our daily Christian walk. The normal Christian life is to walk under an unclouded heaven with the ungrieved, unquenched Holy Spirit filling our lives. If and when a cloud does come across our pathway and we SENSE that fellowship has been interrupted because of some sin in thought, word or deed. This sense of conviction is part of the discipline of God. Our responsibility at that moment in time is to seek the cleansing that is afforded through the cross of our Lord Jesus Christ (1 Jn. 1:9). If we persist in walking in darkness, then the discipline may be more severe. For example, there is a solemn passage in 1 John 5:14-17 which you need to study very carefully. The Apostle tells us there that there is a sin leading to death and if that sin is persisted in, then God has to take drastic measures. You will remember that the Corinthians were guilty

of this kind of sin (see 1 Cor. 11:30) and then follows the words: *"If we would judge ourselves we would not be judged"* (vs. 31). But what I am stressing is the daily walk with God where in love and grace He convicts us when we are out of fellowship and we need to repent and put things right. We forget that repentance is a lifestyle!..."[15]

So to underline what Dr. Stephen F. Olford said we must confess any sin that the Holy Spirit convicts our hearts with and do it immediately! This way, we can have restored fellowship with the Author of our souls. Our problem often is, after we sin, guilt and shame keep us from turning immediately back to God. God is more eager for us to get right with Him than we are! Satan loves to taunt us with our sins in an attempt to keep us from returning to the Father with a contrite heart. So remember, when sin brings a dark cloud over the relationship between you and God act immediately and confess it. Stephen Olford used to tell me when the Holy Spirit would bring a sin to his mind he would pray immediately the following words, "Nail it, Lord, nail it!"

We should do the same! There is great benefit found for a believer in a season of self-examination under the prodding light of the Holy Spirit. If you desire a more intimate walk with God take the time to do the following:

1) Ask God to reveal your heart to you.

The word of God says this about the heart: *"The heart is deceitful above all things, and desperately wicked: who can know it?"* (Jer. 17:9). Ask the Holy Spirit to shine His spotlight of truth upon your heart and reveal to you anything that is an offense to God. Ask God to show you what there is in your life that is a hindrance to having a deeper walk with Him. This can only be done in much prayer and study of the Written Word of God. God will speak to you through His Word and by His Spirit. To hear His voice one must linger and tarry there with Him.

---

15   Personal letter by Stephen F. Olford.

2) Ask God to fill you with the Holy Spirit

A believer is given the Spirit of God when he or she is born again; however, we are leaky buckets and must be continually filled. Remember, there is one baptism but many fillings. D. L. Moody had to learn this; his associate R. A. Torrey taught this concept: that we need to be 'touched by the Holy Spirit" just as the early Apostles were told by Jesus to "tarry in the city of Jerusalem" until they received power from on high.

In fact, one morning D. L. Moody and R. A. Torrey were out riding in a buggy just a few streets down from Moody's home in Northfield, MA. They were discussing the Northfield conference that was then going on where thousands came to hear the Word of God preached and taught by various Bible teachers. Regarding the teachers at the conference Moody commented:

D. L. Moody once said to R. A. Torrey, "Oh, why will they split hairs? Why don't they see that this is just the one thing that they themselves need? They are good teachers, they are wonderful teachers, and I am so glad to have them here; but why will they not see that the baptism with the Holy Ghost [that is, the filling of the Spirit] is just the one touch that they themselves need."[16]

Moody had received "power from on High" and it transformed his ministry. Why do we seek to live the Christian life in our own carnal power of the flesh? It is an impossible task; but when the Holy Spirit takes over we no longer walk in the flesh but "by the Spirit." This way we can say with the Apostle Paul, *"I am crucified with Christ; nevertheless I live; yet not I, but Christ liveth in me: and the life which I now live in the flesh I live by the faith of the Son of God, who loved me, and gave Himself for me"* (Gal. 2:20).

If you are a teacher or preacher of the Word of God and you do not know about this anointing then your teaching or preaching lacks power. You may have a winsome personality, a

---

16   Roger Martin, <u>R. A. Torrey: Apostle of Certainty</u>. (Murfreesboro: Sword of the Lord Publishers) p. 118.

powerful and dramatic voice, an ability to make people laugh, and a way with words. But if you lack unction from on high, your spoken words are merely words spoken by man and have no life transforming power to them; they will not convict the heart and transform lives.

It is the person filled with the Spirit of God and touched by the power of God whose utterances will have the needed effect upon hearers: *"And I will give them one heart, and I will put a new spirit within you; and I will take the stony heart out of their flesh, and will give them a heart of flesh"* (Ezek. 11:19).

If you wish to walk with God as Enoch did, if you desire a deeper walk with Him, then you must seek Him more fully. This is especially true for God's appointed servants. Listen to what E. M. Bounds has to say about "Unction, the Mark of True Gospel Preaching":

> "Unction is that indefinable, indescribable something which an old, renowned Scotch preacher describes thus: 'There is sometimes somewhat in preaching that cannot be ascribed either to matter or expression, and cannot be described what it is, or from whence it cometh, but with a sweet violence it pierceth into the heart and affections and comes immediately from the Lord; but if there be any way to obtain such a thing, it is by the heavenly disposition of the speaker.'

> "We call it unction. It is this unction which makes the word of God 'quick and powerful, and sharper than any two-edged sword, piercing even to the dividing asunder of soul and spirit, and of the joints and marrow, and a discerner of the thoughts and intents of the heart.' It is this unction which gives the words of the preacher such point, sharpness, and power, and which creates such friction and stir in many a dead congregation...This divine unction is the feature which separates and distinguishes true gospel preaching from all other methods of presenting

the truth, and which creates a wide spiritual chasm between the preacher who has it and the one who has it not. It backs and impregnates revealed truth with all the energy of God. Unction is simply putting God in His own word and on His own preacher."[17]

3) Ask God to reveal His plans and purposes for your life

You may be in a rut and away from God right now–you are at a place where you are ready to get serious with Him. Or you may be in a routine with Him where all your effort, prayers, and service are works of the flesh and there is no attendant power associated with them. You may be seeking His face on a important area of your life or perhaps a career move. At any length you are ready to do business with God! Why not pray specific prayers which ask Him pointedly to reveal Himself to you on the area of seeking? The best way to do this is to ask Him to reveal His plans and purposes for your life, your life in the very present now. His Word tells us, *"For I know the thoughts that I think toward you, saith the LORD, thoughts of peace, and not of evil, to give you an expected end"* (Jer. 29:11).

God may be preparing you for greater things! For larger work! For more useful service! How will you realize what that greater usefulness is unless you specifically seek His face in prayer? God had great plans for Enoch: He blessed his bloodline; He gave him visions of future glory; He translated him to Heaven! God has a specific plan for you as well. But to go deeper with Him, to have a more intimate walk with Him you must pursue Him. You must seek Him. But first you must remove the barriers in your life that are blocking communication with Him. *"Nevertheless there are good things found in thee, in that thou hast taken away the groves out of the land, and hast prepared thine heart to seek God"* (2 Chron. 19:3). Also once the barriers are removed and we are cleansed we must seek His face in prayer for direction: *"I would seek unto God, and unto God would I commit my cause"* (Job 5:8). And again we see this in the following passage of Scripture, *"When Thou saidst, Seek ye my face; my heart said*

---

17   E. M. Bounds, <u>The Complete Works of E. M. Bounds On Prayer.</u> (Grand Rapids: Baker Books, 2004) p. 478.

unto Thee, Thy face, LORD, will I seek" (Ps. 27:8).

Good things come to those who dwell with the Lord! The one who walks with God walks like no other! He or she will do greater things for God and for man!

In the next chapter we will contemplate entering His presence.

Learning to pray is no light undertaking. If prayer is the greatest achievement on earth, we may be sure it will call for a discipline that corresponds to its power. The school of prayer has its conditions and demands. It is a forbidden place to all but those of set purpose and resolute heart...The reason so many people do not pray is because of its cost. The cost is not so much in the sweat of agonizing supplication as in the daily fidelity to the life of prayer. It is the acid test of devotion. Nothing in the life of faith is so difficult to maintain.

—Samuel Chadwick

CHAPTER TEN

ENTERING HIS PRESENCE

Before entering the court of an earthly monarch one first prepares himself. One may ask himself, "Are my clothes clean and presentable? Is my hair combed neatly? I must look my best for I am to meet a king!" Also, in the days of old it was a custom to bow before the King. And when it was time to leave the King's presence one would bow and walk backwards so not to turn one's back to his Highness. Some had ended up in prison by turning their back upon their King as they exited the throne room! So first and foremost of a kingly visit was the attitude of respect and reverence.

If such care was taken to enter and exit an earthly royal court, how much more care and concern should we exercise in approaching our heavenly King! Just the thought of it should make us tremble in awe of His Majesty! God is holy. We are sinners. We access Him only through the Son—Jesus.

Jesus is our Forerunner. A forerunner is a small boat which goes before the larger ship to tread the water checking for barrier reefs and other hidden dangers–leading the larger ship safely to the harbor. In the Old Testament the High Priest once a year entered the Holy of Holies on the Day of Atonement and presented the sacrifice for the sins of the people.

Jesus is our High Priest who has gone before us to prepare the way to the Father through His shed blood for the remission of sins. Once we better understand the cost involved of our having access to God in prayer the more we tend to appreciate it! Prayer is something to be treasured not something to be trampled over with carelessness. How carelessly we often pray! God is not "our pal" who we casually call upon anytime we want to and get His attention. I believe He doesn't even hear some of the prayers offered to Him in this careless way. It is only through His grace and mercy that we are even saved from the eternal torments of hell. We error when we fall into a too-casual relationship with the Most High and Creator of the Universe.

It makes me cringe to hear a minister pray from the pulpit in a careless and casual manner as if he and God are just great big friends and the conversation differs little from one carried on in the hallway with one of the church deacons. God forgive us! It is no wonder that God does not answer some of our "casual and careless" prayers. Prayer costs. It cost God His own dear Son. It cost Jesus His own precious blood for us to have access to the Father. Prayer is not something to be taken lightly. This is the first thing we must realize before entering His Presence.

There was a man by the name of Edward Payson who was a pastor in Portland, Maine during the Nineteenth century. He was known as "Praying Payson of Portland" because when he died there was found by his bedside two grooves in the wooden slats of the floor—grooves made by his knees from constant prayer! Regarding prayer the following was found in his diary:

> "December 29th, 1810. Felt the blessed effects of casting all my cares upon him who careth for me. In family prayer, was most unusually drawn out towards God, and felt as much like an inhabitant of heaven as I ever expect to feel here. All earthly objects were swallowed up; self appeared to be nothing, and God to be all in all. Felt as if my time on earth would be short. I was in a strait betwixt the two, having a desire to depart and be with Christ, and yet wishing to stay, that I might tell others what a precious Saviour he is. But the Lord's will be done. Welcome any thing which he pleases to send."[18]

---

18   Edward Payson, <u>The Complete Works of Edward Payson</u>, Volume One. (Harrisonburg: Sprinkle Publications, 1987) p. 202.

We see that "Praying Payson" did not enter the prayer closet carelessly. He knew the price and cost of his redemption. He prayed with a sense of awe.

So should we. The life of a born again believer is somewhat of a journey, a test, and a battle. We will be rewarded in heaven for how well we accomplish all three. We will be rewarded by how faithfully we walk on our journey as pilgrims here on earth; we will be rewarded by how well we act in obedience to God during the time of our test here on earth; and we will be rewarded by how bravely we fight the battle of the Christian life. All of the aforementioned are steeped in prayer. How much failure or success we have depends solely upon our prayer life! If only we truly realized this important truth!

We must keep before us the cost of our redemption. Prayer is a privilege. The entire Christian life is to be lived via the cross. The cross must be applied daily to put to death our sinful desires and it must be applied to our prayer time. We must crucify our pride, our ambition, our self-preservation, and approach God with humility and thankfulness for what He has done in our lives. Our entire prayer life can be transformed with this knowledge.

If we are to enter His presence and encounter Him we must crawl there in brokenness. If we desire to experience His manifest Presence in our prayer life we must understand the following verse of Scripture: *"For thus saith the high and lofty One that inhabiteth eternity, whose name is Holy; I dwell in the high and holy place, with him also that is of a contrite and humble spirit, to revive the spirit of the humble, and to revive the heart of the contrite ones."* (Isa. 57:15).

This is the path to prayer. This is the way to enter His presence. In the next chapter we will look at the joy of walking with God!

As we tread the gospel road together, we take hold of their arm in affection; and we take hold of God for them in supplication. Both these relationships—the affection and the supplication—were so natural to Paul: again and again they are seen in his fellowship especially with his beloved converts.

With some of them, his prayer is weighted with burden—their need is so great, their progress is so disappointing. With these Philippians it is all so different. His prayer for them arises in sheer "joy". They are journeying to heaven along the Joy Way: and even their friends' prayers breathe the happy atmosphere.
                                            —Guy H. King

CHAPTER ELEVEN:
THE WALK OF JOY

There are some things in life that cannot be stolen. Our health can be stolen, our wealth can be stolen, and our loved ones can be stolen away. But our joy in Christ cannot be stolen—not even by the Devil himself. When one walks with God in an intimate relationship like Enoch of old one finds in himself a perpetual joy that no one or no thing can steal away.

No matter our present circumstance in life, no matter how dark and gloomy it may presently be—there is a joy that can be found in a close walk with God. It is a joy that can be found no other way. A human love relationship cannot compare to this heavenly joy. A greatest dream fulfilled cannot compare to this heavenly joy.

The dictionary's definition of joy is: "joy n. 1. Intense or elated happiness. 2. A source of great pleasure. v. To rejoice."[19]

That is man's definition of "joy." Let us turn to the Bible to see how joy is described there. *"...for the joy of the LORD is your strength"* (Neh. 8:10b). We see how joy is described by Nehemiah—we get our strength in the *"joy of the LORD."* Next we see, *"He shall pray unto God, and He will be favorable unto him: and he shall see his face with joy"* (Job 33:26). So when we pray the very presence of God brings us joy!

King David had the very same thoughts when he wrote, *"Thou wilt show me the path of life: in Thy presence is fulness of joy;*

---

19 The American Heritage Dictionary. (New York: Dell Publishing) p. 461.

at Thy right hand there are pleasures forevermore." (Ps. 16:11).

A walk with God truly is a "Joy Way" to coin a phrase from Guy King, an English preacher. In fact, when we follow God we have a promise of joy: *"For God giveth to a man that is good in his sight wisdom, and knowledge, and joy"* (Eccl. 2:26).

Not only is a walk with God a present joy there is a future joy as well for the good and faithful servant of the King! We see this in the following verse, *"His lord said unto him, Well done, thou good and faithful servant: thou hast been faithful over a few things, I will make thee ruler over many things: enter thou into the joy of thy lord"* (Matt. 25:21). Joy in the here and now! Joy in the evermore!

And no matter our circumstances we are to say with the Apostle Paul, *"Rejoice in the Lord always: and again I say, Rejoice"* (Phil. 4:4). Paul wrote this while in chains sitting in a cold, dark, prison!

Our joy cannot be stolen no matter our trials in life. There will be times of sorrow and grief; times of great loss and disappointment; times where we are laid low by the pressures of life and the world and we are not experiencing happiness during those times—but we still can rest in our joy in the Lord. In fact, trials and tribulations force us to go to Him in utter desperation and it is there, in those often trying times that we find Him and experience the greatest degrees of joy!

So a walk with God is a joy no one can steal away! Even in our darkest trials we have this promise of Scripture: *"Weeping may endure for a night, but joy cometh in the morning"* (Ps. 30:5). We have hope as believers. A hope that the world does not share. A hope that can only come from God. When we walk with God our lives take on new meaning. We have a new purpose! And we find a new joy. And the more we walk with Him, the deeper that joy goes into our hearts! Till we can sing with Charles Wesley in his hymn "O for a Thousand Tongues":

He breaks the power of canceled sin,
He sets the prisoners free;
His blood can make the foulest clean;
His blood availed for me.

Hear Him, ye deaf; His praise, ye dumb,
Your loosened tongues employ;
Ye blind, behold your Saviour come;
And leap, ye lame, for joy.

Saturday, June 2, 1739:

"...preached in the evening to about ten thousand at Hackney...Before I went out to preach, I was very sick and weak; but power was given me from above, so that I continued preaching for an hour and a half. It rained some considerable time, but almost all were unmoved; and I was so enlarged by talking of the love and free grace of Jesus Christ, that I could have continued my discourse till midnight. This promise, *'They that wait on the Lord shall renew their strength,'* is fulfilled in me daily."

—George Whitefield

AFTERWORD:
WAITING ON GOD

We must remember that to walk with God effectively we must learn to wait for Him. He does not show up when we snap our fingers. He is not a genie at our command. He is a holy God who dwells in eternity and who deigns to meet those who love His Son and are of a contrite and humble heart.

When we pray we must not rush into His Presence. First, we must acknowledge Him and worship Him. We must thank Him for all the blessings He has given us. We must align our hearts with heaven and be able to say with the Psalmist: *"Bless the LORD, O my soul: and all that within me, bless his holy name. Bless the LORD, O my soul, and forget not all his benefits: who forgiveth all thine iniquities; who healeth all thy diseases; who redeemeth thy life from destruction; who crowneth thee with lovingkindness and tender mercies; who satisfieth thy mouth with good things; so that thy youth is renewed like the eagle's"* (Ps. 103:1-5).

Waiting upon God is time well spent. When we prepare our hearts and minds to enter the throne room of the Almighty there is expectation in the air! No matter what our present circumstances may be we can stand on the promise of God that: *"They that wait upon the LORD shall renew their strength; they shall mount up with wings as eagles; they shall run, and not be weary; and they shall walk, and not faint."* (Isa. 40:31)

There is a key to finding God in the wee small hours of the morning: that is the wait. It is the time spent preparing our hearts and minds to meet Him. Do not rush into your quiet time.

Some pearls on this are found in a little booklet written by Stephen F. Olford, entitled, "Manna in the Morning."

Dr. Olford's advice on "the wait" are priceless. He writes:

> "The first rule is waiting. Samuel Chadwick says, 'Hurry is the death of prayer.' You can get more from the Lord in five minutes spent unhurriedly than in thirty-five minutes with your eye on the clock.
> "Hush yourself in His presence. Wait until the glory of His presence seems to come upon you. Seek the power of concentration. Seek cleansing. Seek the illumination of the Spirit. Above all, seek to consciously come into His presence.
> "From waiting go on to reading. Read the Word of God. I believe with George Muller that you can never pray aright until He has spoken to you from His Word."[20]

Enoch walked with God, *"and he was not."* You can walk with God and be changed as well! God may not translate you physically to heaven like He did with old Enoch but when you walk with Him you may be sure He will transport you to heavenly places! Your heart will sing a new song! Your life will have a new purpose!

When you walk with God you are embarking upon an adventure that this world can never match. When you walk with God you are separating yourself from the masses of humanity, even from the majority of believers, and are entering the most exciting phase of your life! Once your walk with God begins it will radically change everything! You will awake with expectation!

Picture the following in your mind: if you have ever owned a dog you know how that faithful animal waits patiently for his master's appearance at the start of the day. My dog lives outside and sits by the back door in the morning waiting for me to come

---

20   Stephen F. Olford, <u>Manna in the Morning.</u> (Memphis: Olford Ministries International) p. 9.

out to see her. There is a look of expectation on her face when she first sees me in the morning: she knows she will be fed and petted. She is happy to see me! Now, imagine God (the Creator of the Universe) waiting expectantly for us as we awake in the morning. God has some wonderful blessings to bestow upon us today and when we meet Him in prayer and enter that close walk with Him that gives Him the opportunity to bless us with His presence and speak to our hearts by His Holy Spirit!

When we fail to show up for our morning walk with Him — He is disappointed. No matter how hard that is for us to fathom it is true. God enjoys a love relationship with us and He draws near to those who draw near to Him. As a matter of fact the blessings that God has for you today are linked directly with this daily walk with Him.

If we fail to have that "quiet time" alone with Him then we miss out on blessings!

All the great Christians in history shared a common denominator: a close walk with God. And when you study their lives in biography you learn that God blessed them immeasurably to the amount of time spent in daily communion with Him. How could a George Mueller run an orphanage with a thousand orphans to clothe and feed and not make his financial needs known to the world? He did not need to beg from others: he met with God each day and told God of his need and God answered each need every time! This faith that George Mueller possessed was strengthened in prayer.

This great faith of Mueller enabled him to comment:

> "How many times we find this expression, *The living God*' (Daniel 6:20), in the Scriptures, and yet it is just this very thing that we are so prone to lose sight of! We know it is written, 'the living God'; but in our daily life there is scarcely anything we lose sight of so much as the fact that God is the living God; that He is now whatever He was three or four thousand

years ago; that He has the same sovereign power, the same saving love toward those who love and serve Him as ever He had, and that He will do for them now what He did for others two, three, four thousand years ago, simply because He is 'the living God,' the Unchanging One. Oh, how we should confide in Him therefore, and in our darkest moments never lose sight of the fact that He is still and ever will be 'the living God.'"[21]

Another man used mightily of God was Charles Spurgeon, the famous British preacher, founder of the famed Metropolitan Tabernacle church in London and Spurgeon's college. If any follower of Christ knew the importance of a daily tryst with God in the morning it was Spurgeon! The smile of heaven was upon Spurgeon's ministry and he had a direct link to heaven each day by an effective walk with God.

Spurgeon had a favorite verse from the Psalms that he often would quote and comment upon which reflected his thoughts on this daily time with the Lord. We see this in the following:

> *"'My voice shalt Thou hear in the morning, O LORD; in the morning will I direct my prayer unto Thee, and will look up.'* (Ps. 5:3). The morning is the gate of the day, and should be well-guarded with prayer. It is one end of the thread on which the day's actions are strung, and should be well-knotted with devotion. If we felt more the majesty of life we would be more careful of its mornings. He who rushes from his bed to his business and does not wait to worship is as foolish as if he had not put on his clothes or cleaned his face, and as unwise as if he dashed into battle without arms or armor. It is ours to bathe in the softly flowing river of communion with God, before the heat of the wilderness and the burden of the way begin to oppress us."[22]

---

21   D. L. Moody, <u>Morning Devotional</u>. (New Kensington: Whitaker House) p. 23.
22   Moody, <u>Morning Devotional</u>. pp. 14, 15.

When we turn our devotion and our needs to God first thing in the morning we can rest upon His precious promise that *"God shall supply all your need according to his riches in glory by Christ Jesus"* (Phil. 4:19).

As we have looked at the lives of great people of faith in both Scripture and history let their examples of holy living and a close walk with God encourage each of us to make it a point to have an impassioned daily walk with Him. As the example of Enoch has spoken to our hearts let it be a model for us to follow! God made the ultimate sacrifice of sending His dear Son to die on a cross for us; to suffer and die so that whoever believes upon Him has eternal life! If God made such a great sacrifice on our behalf, is it too much to ask of us a sacrifice of our time spent in daily devotion with Him? When we realize the cost of our salvation we cannot but fall at the Master's Feet each day in thanksgiving and praise, worship and prayer! The more time we spend with Him the more we delight in Him! Is this not true?

When we spend time with God each day our thoughts and focus take on heavenly dimensions. Our daily purpose takes on deeper meaning! Even the look in our eyes will be different.

Those that walk with God have a certain look in their eyes. There is a photograph of C. T. Studd taken right before he died. He is in the bush of Africa, where he has spent the last years of his life bringing the gospel to the natives of that land. The camera is focused on his face, especially his eyes. He has a far-away look in his eyes—as if he is peering into the very portals of heaven! Eternity had been stamped upon his eyelids and he lived his life for others.

When we walk with God we stop living for ourselves. When we walk with Him our entire earthly focus is changed! As the face of Moses was changed into a radiance from the time he spent with God atop the mountain, so, too, our own lives will be transformed by lingering in the presence of God!

Waiting upon God and walking with God—what marvelous themes! Let us join in praise with the words of William Cowper, who wrote the following hymn:

WALKING WITH GOD

O for a closer walk with God,
A calm and heavenly frame,
A light to shine upon the road
That leads me to the Lamb!

Where is the blessedness I knew
When first I saw the Lord?
Where is the soul-refreshing view
Of Jesus and His word?

What peaceful hours I once enjoy'd!
How sweet their memory still!
But they have left an aching void,
The world can never fill.

Return, O holy Dove, return,
Sweet messenger of rest:
I hate the sins that made Thee mourn,
And drove Thee from my breast.

The dearest idol I have known,
Whate'er that idol be,
Help me to tear it from Thy throne,
And worship only Thee.

So shall my walk be close with God,
Calm and serene my frame;
So purer light shall mark the road
That leads me to the Lamb.
          —William Cowper

As we wait on God in a close walk with Him let us be ever mindful that it is always a supreme privilege to do so! Let us never take it for granted nor let its sweetness fade. As our years go on let us tread that narrow pathway that leads to Him. Our whole life should be a non-stop walk with Him!

There is no greater joy than waiting upon the Lord and entering into close fellowship with Him. May your own walk with God be Enoch-like in nature and heavenly in purpose! As you follow Him remember to listen and obey. I promise you on the authority of Scripture your life will never be the same. May God bless you as you pursue Him passionately!

> May your walk with Him be guarded,
> A priority in your life;
> May you seek Him early in the morning,
> For the rest of your life.
> May it make you more like Jesus,
> Increasing more with each new day.
> As you walk with God Almighty,
> Let Him lead the way.
> —E. A. Johnston

APPENDIX

Walking with God is not an automatic. Just because we are believers does not mean we will automatically have a close and personal walk with God–this must be developed. As it takes time to build a friendship here on earth with our earthly friends imagine the care and priority of working towards building a close walk with our heavenly Father! We must remind ourselves that age and years in Christ as believers does not automatically give us a close walk with Him; we know many believers who are mature in their years but not in their walk. We encounter senior citizens in Christ who are shamefully carnal and babes. A walk with God must be developed with as much care as one would tend a garden; it must be watered and visited regularly. Our walk with God must be watered by our tears of gratitude and thankfulness for what He has done for us! Our walk with God must be daily, moment by moment, lest we grow cold towards Him and allow sin, self, and the world come between us! Our hearts are evil, deceitful, and have a natural tendency to drift away from God through apathy, indifference, formality, and hardening.

We have this warning from Scripture:*"While it is said, Today if ye will hear his voice, harden not your hearts, as in the provocation"* (Heb. 3:15).

Unfortunately, many Christians today are suffering from heart disease; not the physical kind but the spiritual kind! How easy it is for our hearts to grow cold and hard towards Him! How easy it is for a sheep to stray from the fold. We can grow careless towards the Lord in many ways. In a friendship with an earthly friend things can come between and cause division or separation: envy, jealousy, pride, anger, bitterness, unforgiveness. In our walk with God there are certain hindrances that can cause us to have a breach with Him. Remember this, if our walk with God has become distant–He did not move! We did! He is always a breath away from us. It is we who hinder our progress with Him. Allow us to examine some of these hindrances and be alert to them as they are often insidious and unnoticeable by us.

Hindrances to walking with God

1) Pride

Pride is an obstacle to walking with God. God will not walk close with a proud and haughty heart. Sadly, a proud person is the last to know this about themselves. God will not and cannot dwell with a proud heart. If you are saved and have the Spirit of Christ in you and remain a proud person you will grieve the Holy Spirit on a regular basis. God only dwells in two places: this is seen in the following verse of Scripture: *"For thus saith the high and lofty One that inhabiteth eternity, whose name is Holy; I dwell in the high and holy place, with him also that is of a contrite and humble spirit, to revive the spirit of the humble, and to revive the heart of the contrite ones"* (Isa. 57:15).

The two places that God dwells is in heaven and with the humble. If we miss this point we miss everything regarding a close and intimate walk with God. Those believers that walk closest with God are the humble and contrite ones. Jesus was born in a humble stable not a proud palace. Our Master washed His disciple's feet with humility. The following verse speaks of this: *"The sacrifices of God are a broken spirit: a broken and a contrite heart, O God, thou wilt not despise"* (Ps. 51:17).

2) Self-righteousness

One of the biggest obstacles to walking in an intimate relationship with God is our self-righteousness. When we are full of self-righteousness it grieves the heart of God. A self-righteous person may be important in his or her own eyes but in the eyes of God we see:

"But we are all as an unclean thing, and all our righteousnesses are as filthy rags; and we all do fade as a leaf; and our iniquities, like the wind, have taken us away"(Isa. 64:6).

Allow me to present an example of how our self-righteousness grieves the heart of God and hinders our walk with Him. I was in a revival meeting in a church which was being led by a out-of-town evangelist. The evangelist was conducting a series of meetings for the week. There was a hindrance to the work of God there in that congregation and on the last night we learned why. A man (an officer of the church) came forward at the end of the message and announced he wished to make a statement to the church body. He said that he had been angry with a man there that week and God had showed him this and he was announcing that it was wrong for him to have been angry at this person. He admitted this in his statement. Then he led the congregation in a flowery prayer and closed the evening service. Rather than feeling the Spirit of God descend on that little church you could feel the Spirit leave. Why? What had grieved Him so?

We feel the answer is in the following: had the leader of the church been repentant, contrite, and broken over his sin God would have flooded that assembly with His presence. God loves a humble and contrite heart and dwells there. Rather, this man was not repentant, contrite, or broken. He was sorry he had felt that way toward another believer but his was not Godly sorrow but fleshly sorrow. It made him look good to be standing up there at the front of the church and say that he was so spiritual that he heard the voice of God convict him of his error in being angry at another believer. His apology was enwrapped with self-righteousness. He was a proud man who acknowledged his wrong but like Esau there was no true repentance of a contrite heart. God did not except his sacrifice that night and there was a coldness in the assembly. Had this man been truly broken over his sin and humble and contrite in front of God, there is no telling how many other believers would have come forward that night with the same confession and brokenness–this is how revival begins!

Our point is if we are not aware of the obstacles that hinder a walk with God how can we avoid them? The following passage of Scripture is a good example of what we have been discussing:

> *"Two men went up into the temple to pray; the one a Pharisee, and the other a publican. The Pharisee stood and prayed thus with himself, God, I thank thee, that I am not as other men are, extortioners, unjust, adulterers, or even as this publican. I fast twice in the week, I give tithes of all that I possess. And the publican, standing afar off, would not lift up so much as his eyes unto heaven, but smote upon his breast, saying, God be mericful to me a sinner. I tell you, this man went down to his house justified rather than the other: for every one that exalteth himself shall be abased; and he that humbleth himself shall be exalted"* (Luke 18:10-14).

3) Lack of Time Spent in the Word of God

Those who seldom read their Bibles will seldom walk with God. How does one get to know the God of the Word if one does not know the Word of God? If watching television consumes more of our time than the study of Scripture we will probably be up to date on the latest craze in Hollywood but we will be out of touch with God. If we are seeking guidance in our life (career, marriage, family, relocation, ministry, etc) the best place to seek that guidance is in the Word of God. God speaks often to His children through His written Word. If we fail to inquire into the Word of God how can we know the heart of God? We get to know God and come to a deeper understanding of Him by meditating and studying His holy Scriptures. We should approach our Bibles with the same thrill of the Psalmist: *"I rejoice at thy word, as one that findeth great spoil"* (Ps. 119:162).The Bible is a book about God's Son–Jesus! When we turn to the word of God we behold the face of the Son of God! When we read our Bibles we see God's heart and plan for mankind! The more time we spend in the Word of God the more we will understand about the God of the Word.

4) Lack of Prayer

Those believers who have a rich prayer life also have a rich walk with God! Show me a man or woman who is a prayer warrior and I will show you a intimate friend of God. Failure to pray is the biggest obstacle between us and God. Enoch walked closely with God because he enjoyed the fellowship and communication he shared with God! If you have a best friend you want to spend time with them. How can you expect God to be your close friend if you do not spend quality time with Him? The greatest saints in history who did the most for God all shared a common denominator—prayer. When George Whitefield and John Wesley awakened a slumbering nation with their preaching in the mid-eighteen century the very gates of hell shook as well! How did they accomplish this? Their success can be tied directly to their "love feasts" in Fetter Lane. What was a "love feast"? This was an entire night given to prayer and fasting by these holy men of God. They literally feasted on God's love all evening! Both Whitefield and Wesley would never have had the power they had in preaching had they not spent long hours in prayer before the throne of their Master. How do we expect to preach with power when we are so derelict in our own prayer time? Powerful preaching is a direct outflow of powerful praying! Our cry should be like that of the Psalmist: *"As the hart panteth after the water brooks, so panteth my soul after thee, O God. My soul thirsteth for God, for the living God: when shall I come and appear before God?"* (Ps. 42:1,2).

Let us learn how to prevail in prayer, travail in prayer, and lay hold of God in prayer! Remember, the more time we spend with Him the better we will know Him.

5) Greed

If you are a greedy person you will not have a close walk with God. Your money is not your money–it is His! Just because you may have tithed 10% last year does not give you a close walk with God. What are you doing with the 90%? Is it furthering missions? Is it going to Bible translation for those languages who still lack the Scripture in their native tongue? Or are you a hoarder. Do you like to hoard your gold? Has God asked you to give some money to His work and you have been disobedient in this area? Are you selfless with money or are you selfish with money? There is enough money in Christian bank accounts and at present to reach this world for Christ and fulfill the Great Commission. Yet, there are 2200 languages that still wait for the Word of God to be translated into their native tongue. Ministries are closing their doors all over the world for lack of funds. There are ministries in your community right now that suffer because Christians fail to give. Greed will kill your walk with God. Jesus had much to say in this regard of hoarding:

> *"The ground of a certain rich man brought forth plentifully: And he thought within himself, saying, What shall I do, because I have no room where to bestow my fruits? And he said, This will I do: I will pull down my barns, and build greater; and there will I bestow all my fruits and my goods. And I will say to my soul, Soul, thou hast much goods laid up for many years; take thine ease, eat, drink, and be merry. But God said unto him, Thou fool, this night thy soul shall be required of thee: then whose shall those things be, which thou hast provided? So is he that layeth up treasure for himself, and is not rich toward God"* (Luke 12:16-21).

6) A Habitual Sin

Do you have a "pet sin" that has a grip on your life? Are you its slave? Do you continue to fall into this sin as a dog returns to its vomit? There is a major difference between confession and repentance. Repentance means turning from a sin completely. When we repeatedly practice a sin over and over again this grieves the heart of God. This is dangerous ground. If you have a lust or habit that controls you and you refuse to give it up for God then God will eventually allow that lust to consume you. If you have a temper and are prone to anger and you do not surrender this sin to God it will eventually wreck havoc upon your home life. Sin leaves a miserable calling card! How many believers trample the blood of Christ and Grace! If you have a habitual sin that you refuse to turn from you will never have a close walk with God. You are only fooling yourself–but you are also harming those around you.

7) Unforgiveness Toward Another

If you have a root of bitterness toward another person and refuse to forgive that person you are out of fellowship with God. A root of bitterness toward another can harden your heart against God. A root of bitterness can make you grow cold spiritually. Jesus had much to say on this subject! *"Therefore if thou bring thy gift to the altar, and there rememberest that thy brother hath aught against thee; leave there thy gift before the altar, and go thy way; first be reconciled to thy brother, and then come and offer thy gift"* (Matt. 5:23-24). *"Likewise, ye husbands, dwell with them according to knowledge, giving honor unto the wife, as unto the weaker vessel, and as being heirs together of the grace of life; that your prayers be not hindered"* (1 Pet. 3:7).

For us to have a unclouded walk with God full of sunshine and His favor we must be watchful and careful to recognize any hindrances that creep into our lives each day and prevent us from fully walking with Him. Removing obstacles! That is what God wants! As we enter a close walk with God let our prayer be the following: *"And shall say, Cast ye up, cast ye up, prepare the way, take up the stumblingblock out of the way of my people"* (Isa. 57:14).

Remember, Satan does not want you to have a close walk with God because he knows if you do you will be a powerful weapon in His hand! Satan will throw stumbling blocks in our way to throw us off track in our fellowship with the Father— but be wise to his ways! Stay as close to the cross as you can this side of heaven and you will enjoy a marvelous walk with the Creator! God bless you.

Bibliography

Each of the following books will take the reader to "the Throne" and help in a close walk with God. Unfortunately, many of these good books are out-of-print but can be found through the internet through used book services. These books are a recommended reading list for any serious believer who desires a closer walk with the Lord.

Austin-Sparks, T. The Works of T. Austin-Sparks. Jacksonville: The SeedSowers,

Baldwin, Lindley. Samuel Morris. Minneapolis: Bethany House, 1942.

Baxter, J. Sidlow. Going Deeper. Grand Rapids: Zondervan Books, 1971.

Blackaby, Henry. Fresh Encounter. Nashville: Broadman & Holman Publishers, 1996.

Bonar, Andrew. Diary and Life. Edinburgh: Banner of Truth, 1984.

Bonar, Andrew. Memoir and Remains of Robert Murray M'Cheyne. Edinburgh: Banner of Truth, 1997.

Bounds, E. M. The Complete Works of E. M. Bounds on Prayer. Grand Rapids: Baker Books, 2004.

Brainerd, David. The Life and Diary of David Brainerd. Grand Rapids: Baker Books, 2001.

Chadwick, Samuel. The Path of Prayer. Fort Washington: Christian Literature Crusade, 2000

Charnock, Stephen. The Existence and Attributes of God, Grand Rapids: Baker Books, 1986.

Crossley, Aaron. The Life and Times of Selina Countess of Huntingdon: Volume 1. Staffs: Tentmaker Publications, 2001.

Crossley, Aaron. The Life and Times of Selina Countess of Huntingdon: Volume 2. Staffs: Tentmaker Publications, 2001.

Drummond, Lewis. Spurgeon Prince of Preachers. Grand Rapids: Kregel Books, 1992.

Finney, Charles. Lectures on Revival. Minneapolis: Bethany Books, 1988.

Fullerton, W. Y. No Ordinary Man: F. B. Meyer. Greenville: Ambassador, 1993.

Goforth, Jonathan. By My Spirit. Elkhart: Bethel Publishing, 1983.

Grubb, Norman. C. T. Studd: Cricketer & Pioneer. Fort Washington: Christian Literature Crusade, 2001.

Grubb, Norman. Rees Howells: Intercessor. Fort Washington: Christian Literature Crusade, 1999.

Gurnall, William. The Christian in Complete Armour. Edinburgh: Banner of Truth, 1995.

Huegel, F. J. Bone of His Bone. Fort Washington: Christian Literature Crusade, 2002.

Johnston, E. A. Return to Me. Port Colborne: Gospel Folio Press, 2007.

MacDonald, William. My Heart, My Life, My All. Port Colborne: Gospel Folio Press, 1997.

MacDonald, William. True Discipleship. Port Colborne: Gospel Folio Press, 2003.

Maxwell, L. E. Born Crucified. Chicago: Moody Press, 1945.

Moody, William. The Life of D. L. Moody. Murfreesboro: Sword of the Lord Publishers.

Murray, Andrew. Absolute Surrender. Orlando: Bridge-Logos, 2005.

Murray, Iain H. Jonathan Edwards A New Biography. Edinburgh: Banner of Truth, 2000.

Olford, Stephen. Not I But Christ. Wheaton: Crossway Books, 1986.

Packer, J. I. <u>Knowing God</u>. Downers Grove: InterVarsity Press, 2006.

Purves, Jock. <u>Fair Sunshine</u>. Edinburgh: Banner of Truth, 1997.

Ravenhill, Leonard. <u>Why Revival Tarries</u>. Minneapolis: Bethany Books.

Rendall, Ted. <u>Fire in the Church</u>. Chicago: Moody Press, 1974.

Roberts, Richard Owen. <u>Repentance: The First Word of the Gospel</u>. Wheaton: Crossway Books, 2002.

Tracy, Joseph. <u>The Great Awakening</u>. Edinburgh: Banner of Truth, 1997.

Whitefield, George. <u>George Whitefield's Journals</u>. Edinburgh: Banner of Truth, 1998.

Woolsey, Andrew. <u>Channel of Revival: A Biography of Duncan Campbell</u>. Edinburgh: Faith Mission, 1982.

WHY GOD USED STEPHEN F. OLFORD

By

Dr. E. A. Johnston

Dr. Stephen F. Olford (1918—2004)

Dr. Stephen F. Olford was an internationally recognized preacher, evangelist and Christian leader as well as the author of numerous books and booklets, and 7 volumes of expository preaching outlines.

His ministry spanned more than 60 years, including pastorates at Duke Street Baptist Church in England (1953 - 1959) and Calvary Baptist Church in New York City (1959 - 1973).

In 1980, he launched the Institute for Biblical Preaching to promote biblical preaching and spiritual revival in an hour when churches everywhere desperately needed" ... refreshing from the presence of the Lord."

There are some choice servants in the kingdom of God whom Heaven smiled upon in a remarkable way and enabled them to be mightily used of God to bring Him glory. These choice servants share a common denominator: a consecrated life in full surrender to the Holy Spirit. One cannot think of Dr. Stephen Olford without acknowledging the power of the Holy Spirit upon his life and ministry. In fact, it was the H?ly Spirit who anointed him and gave him such powerful unction in the pulpit. But this "power in the pulpit" comes with a price, a sacrifice, a life of prayer, surrender-cross bearing. Because of his holy walk and his priority on prayer, Stephen Olford knew God and he could preach Christ crucified with power-power that would transform the hearts of those who heard him preach with such Spirit-anointed power. He was a man small in stature yet when he ascended the pulpit and began to proclaim God's message he appeared to be a giant speaking to mere mortals.

Stephen Olford lived life in accord with the following verse of Scripture: *"I am crucified with Christ: nevertheless I live; yet not I, but Christ liveth in me: and the life which I now live in the flesh I live by the faith of the Son of God, who loved me, and gave Himself far me"* (Gal.2:20)

One word sums up the life and ministry of Dr. Stephen F. Olford more that any other and that is: Lordship. The mess-age of the crucified life under the Lordship of Christ preached in full- that is, Christ not only saves from the penalty of sin but Christ saves us also from the power of sin. This does not mean sinless perfection; it means having the power to live a holy life. It's the message of full salvation in Christ! The following summation of why God used Stephen

Olford therefore is in the form of an acrostic which spells LORDSHIP. God used Stephen F. Olford for the following reasons:

LORDSHIP

LOVE OF OTHERS

OBEDIENCE TO CHRIST

REVIVAL BURDEN

DEVOTIONAL LIFE

SURRENDERED TO GOD'S WILL

HOLY WALK

INTERNATIONAL FOCUS

PASSION FOR PREACHING

LOVE FOR OTHERS

Dr. Olford not only had a burden for the ost, he had the passion for helping believers live the victorious Christian life, on his desk in his private study lay a little plaque that read: "others. "He knew he was a servant serving others, all to the glory of God.

OBEDIENCE TO CHRIST

One cannot attain greatness and accomplish much for God unless one is obedient to the commanding officer. God knew that He could trust Stephen Olford with much because of his instant obedience to the Master's voice. Dr. Olford possessed a remarkable ability to be

"sensitive" to the leading of the Holy Spirit-and he always sought to yield in obedience to Him.

REVIVAL BURDEN

Stephen Olford literally had a heart cry for revival. God honored this in his life by displaying His Manifest Presence among His people on many occasions. One can think of the revival on the campus of Wheaton College, which began with a broken Stephen Olford, out of bed all evening, and on his knees crying to God in prayer. Stephen Olford was a man of revival.

DEVOTIONAL LIFE

Stephen Olford was a man of prayer. He knew the importance and priority of the "Quiet Time," the time set apart for God in prayer early in the morning. His little booklet, Manna In The Morning, is a testimony to how he ordered and prioritized his time with the Lord. The great power he had in preaching was an overflow of the time spent on his knees in prayer.

SURRENDERED TO GOD'S WILL

It has been said of Stephen Olford that he lived his life in the "springtime" meaning that he always was pressing on with urgency to serve His Master with a great expectation as to what God would do! But one cannot have this life of faith without a life of surrender. Christ resided on the throne of his life in complete Lordship.

HOLY WALK

Stephen Olford maintained a holy walk with God throughout his life and God honored this in His servant. Holiness was the most important thing in his relationship to God. On the wall of his private study was a plaque which quoted his hero, Robert Murray M'Cheyne, which read, "Lord, make me as holy as a saved sinner can be!" Stephen Olford was very much like M'Cheyne in this regard. He had a holy manner about him in and out of the pulpit. This holy walk allowed him to exhibit authority which was a demonstration of the Spirit of God in the man.

INTERNATIONAL FOCUS

Dr. Olford was an international man who served and represented a global God. His ministry was not local but international-reaching across the globe; from Africa to Japan, from Italy to Trinidad. Far too many of us limit God by limiting our fields of focus;

With Stephen Olford the world was open territory to proclaim the gospel of Christ!

PASSION FOR PREACHING

Few men have exhibited such a life devoted o the "preaching ministry." When it came to preaching, Stephen Olford had a "fire in his belly" for all to see! Few men have preached with such God-anointed power and authority in expository preaching. He knew the critical times in which he lived, where expository preaching had to be proclaimed and taught because of what was in the balance if this form of preaching were to die out. Teaching expository preaching to others as well as modeling expository preaching himself -was a passion for him. Many great preachers themselves were challenged when listening to Stephen Olford preach.

All of the aforementioned spell: Lordship. If one desires to know why God used Stephen F. Olford so mightily, the answer can be found in that word.

SOME BOOKS, BOOKLETS AND MINISTRY RESOURCES BY STEPHEN OLFORD

Anointed Expository Preaching...equips and encourages preachers and Bible teachers to respect their calling and minister God's Word, in the power and anointing of the Spirit. (Co-authored with Dr. David Olford)

Windows of Wisdom ... beautifully illustrated devotional study of Proverbs, written our of the crucible of the author's battle with cancer.

The Grace of Giving ... comprehensive, scriptural study of financial stewardship, with application questions in every chapter.

The Tabernacle (Camping with God) ... an in-depth study of every aspect of this little-understood part of the Old Testament - the "tent" in which God came down to camp with His people.

BOOKLETS BY STEPHEN OLFORD

Manna in the Morning... classic Stephen Olford tract encouraging the Christ-follower to have a daily time of devotion alone with the Lord. this is a must, he writes, for daily spiritual sustenance.

Becoming a Child of God... what is involved in becoming a "child of God"? Basing his answer on John 1: 12-13, Dr. Olford discusses the implications of a person's new life in Christ. Booklet concludes with "9 Rights" to help a new believer walk as a child of God.

Encounter with Anxiety ... based on a study of Philippians 4:6-7, Dr. Olford provides a scriptural response to the age-old problem of anxiety.

Other Olford Resources

Deluxe Olford Preaching CD (WordSearch) a multimedia CD featuring Dr. Olford's 7 Expository Preaching Volumes, 12 Olford books, video introduction, and 5-part audio series "Meet These Men"

Reign of Righteousness" **(Romans)** **a** stunning "live" expository preaching by Stephen Olford through Paul's epistle to the Romans - 52 messages in 4 CD albums, with message notes.

Olford Audio Seminar.This complete course resource is like a home study version of an Olford preaching event in Memphis. Contains 4-paRt audio series "Anointed Biblical Preaching & Teaching," Olford books Anointed Expository Preaching and Not I, But Christ, along with course notes and message outlines.

For more information on these and other preaching resources, visit the Stephen Olford Center website at www.olford.org.

ABOUT THE AUTHOR

Dr. E. A. Johnston is a fellow of the Stephen Olford Institute for Biblical Preaching and is actively involved in Bible teaching and disciple-making. He is the author of many books, including a new work on George Whitefield, the great English evangelist.

BOOKS BY E. A. JOHNSTON

1. *"A Heart Awake: The Authorized Biography of J. Sidlow Baxter"* Foreword by Adrian Rogers (Baker Books, Grand Rapids; 2005).

2. *"Realities Of Revival"* Foreword by Stephen F. Olford (Gospel Folio Press, Canada; 2005).

3. *"No Turning Back"* (Gospel Folio Press, Canada; 2005).

4. *"The Master's Plan: Unfolding God's Blueprint For Your Life"* (Gospel Folio Press, Canada; 2006).

5. **"Know The Book: Bible Survey At A Glance"** (Gospel Folio Press, Canada; 2007).

6. *"Jua Kitabu: Tazamo la Biblia"* Know The Book translated into the Swahili by missionary G. I. Harlow (Everyday Publications, Canada; 2007).

7. *"Return To Me: Entering A Right Relationship With God"* (Gospel Folio Press, Canada; 2007).

8. *"Are You In The Book Of Life?"* (Gospel Folio Press, Canada; 2008).

9. *"Call To Revival"* Foreword By Colin Peckham (Gospel Folio Press, Canada; 2008).

10. *"The Church In Revival"* Foreword By Richard Owen Roberts (Gospel Folio Press, Canada; 2008).

11. *"Olford On Scroggie: Stephen Olford's Notes on the Sermon Outlines of Graham*

Scroggie" Co-authored with Stephen Olford (Gospel Folio Press, Canada; 2008).

12.   *"George Whitefield A Definitive Biography Two Volumes In One"* (The Old Paths Publications, Inc., 2024).

13.   *"Asahel Nettleton Revival Preacher"* Foreword By John Thornbury, Preface By Richard Owen Roberts (The Old Paths Publications, Inc., 2024).

14.   *"Sermons For Revival"* (The Old Paths Publications, Inc., 2024).

15.   *"A Noble Company Biographical Essays on Notable Particular Baptists in America Volume 11: Portrait of Rolfe Barnard"* (The Old Paths Publications, Inc., 2024).

And others. See:

E. A. Johnston Books
(theoldpathspublications.com)

9 798990 327313